an illustrated guide to
Dream
meaning

an illustrated guide to
Dream
meaning

sasha fenton

GRAMERCY BOOKS · NEW YORK

This 2001 edition is published by Gramercy Books™, an imprint of Random House Value Publishing, Inc., 280 Park Avenue, New York, NY 10017, by arrangement with D&S Books, Cottage Meadow, Bocombe, Parkham, Bideford, Devon, England, EX39 5PH.

Gramercy Books™ and design are trademarks of Random House Value Publishing, Inc.

Printed in Singapore.

Random House
New York ● Toronto ● London ● Sydney ● Auckland
http://www.randomhouse.com/

A catalog record for this title is available from the Library of Congress

ISBN: 0–517–16399–3

987654321

contents

introduction

Last night I dreamed that I had a mobile phone jammed against my left ear. Someone was screaming instructions down it, and while I couldn't understand the screeching voice, I was perfectly well aware that it was hurting my ear. Was this a message from the gods? A significator of my psychological condition? Was this dream foretelling the future? Not at all. As it happens, I have an ear infection at the moment, so I guess that my brain was trying to make sense of the pain in my ear! This may be a mundane and logical explanation of a particular dream, but there are many other kinds of dream experience.

My mobile-phone nightmare had a logical reason.

CAN YOU CHOOSE YOUR DREAMS?

There is a technique, called "lucid dreaming," in which you settle on the dream that you want to have and concentrate on it before falling asleep. The purpose is to allow your mind to work on the subject or the problem contained in the dream. If you can do this, the dream will not take place soon after you have fallen asleep, but an hour or two before you wake up. Some people can do this, others can't.

DREAMS AND HISTORY

It is probable that people have discussed their dreams from the dawn of history. Certainly, the Bible and other early texts contain stories about important or prophetic dreams, the most famous being Joseph's dreams of future famine in Egypt and Jacob's dream of a ladder leading to heaven.

Dreaming is a universal experience. Every race and culture in the world tells stories about dreams, and dream books are not confined to the Western world. Such books have existed for centuries in the Middle and Far East, especially in Iran, where dreams are considered to be important indicators of future events. Many African tribes believe strongly in the messages contained in dreams, and some Africans have even perfected ways of sending messages telepathically to relatives who live some distance away, passing their dreams along a kind of dream highway.

Dreams of falling are classic dreams.

DREAMS AND PSYCHOANALYSIS

Sigmund Freud (1856–1939) and Carl Gustav Jung (1875–1961), the founders of modern psychoanalysis, were the first medical men to take dreams seriously, concluding that they revealed a lot about the state of a patient's mind. Jung suggested to his patients that if they awoke during the night with a vivid dream in mind, they should write it down straightaway, because it is difficult to recall a dream later.

Classic dreams of insecurity that children and young people frequently experience are those of falling, especially falling down stairs. Another common dream is of finding oneself in the street dressed in one's underclothes. Yet another is of being hungry and not having any money with which to buy food.

R.E.M. SLEEP

Dr. Nathanial Kleitman and his student Dr. Eugene Aserinsky discovered R.E.M. (rapid eye movement) sleep in 1953. Their research has shown us that dreams occur during set periods when our eyes appear to move about and our muscles twitch. These R.E.M. periods occur after each hour and a half of deep sleep and last for about 20 minutes. This is why we sometimes wake up, become aware that we are dreaming, and then fall asleep again.

Those who swear that they never dream are wrong: they just don't remember their dreams. Fortunately, most people do recall some of their dreams, and if you are one you will find this book a fascinating reference tool with which to discover the meanings of your nocturnal voyages.

Chase dreams indicate insecurity or anxiety.

A lovely dream of a happy family is heart-warming.

WHAT ARE DREAMS?

Dreams fall into a number of different categories. Some are merely your mind's way of clearing space, much like organizing and deleting files on a computer. Others show that the mind is troubled and feels that life is spiraling out of control. Trying to grasp things that are out of reach, rushing to catch something that moves away, dreams of being in a maze, and other disturbing dreams all show that the dreamer is striving to achieve the unachievable.

These dreams are an indication that too many pressures are piling up on a person and that he or she needs to get a grip and take control of life.

Dreams may warn against laziness, vanity,

Dreaming of prosperity is common.

Experiments were made into studying while asleep.

keeping bad company, wasting money, accepting the wrong job, and much more. Dreams may foretell happiness, prosperity, meeting the right lover, having children, moving to a nicer house, and more besides. Almost half of the dreams that show the dreamer faces or people involve strangers, although another large group of dreams involves family and friends. Every kind of human activity is seen in dreams, and every kind of emotion can be explored.

SLEEP LEARNING

Some years ago, investigations were carried out into sleep learning, where tape recordings were

A "contrary" dream means the opposite of what it says.

played to a sleeper in the hope that he or she would be able to absorb the information given while they were sleeping. These experiments didn't really work, because the sleeping mind is more concerned with sorting out what is already inside it than in taking more information on board.

Some people wake up with a clear answer to a puzzling problem, which shows that the mind continues to work during sleep. Successful lucid-dreamers are able to tune their brains in a particular direction before falling asleep in order to encourage this process.

PREDICTIVE DREAMS

Some dreams may foretell the future by showing the dreamer exactly what will happen, but most do so symbolically. The human mind resonates to symbols that have a specific meaning, and a book like this will help you to recognize these dream symbols and understand what they are trying to tell you.

Many symbols are fairly obvious. For example, dreaming of wandering around barefoot and in rags suggests that your expectations will come to nothing, that you are walking on dangerous ground, or are surrounded by evil influences. Others are not so obvious. One brilliant dream interpreter on a phone-in radio show once told a caller that her dream about ants meant that she had an extremely difficult mother-in-law who was driving her up the wall. The astonished listener agreed that this was exactly the case!

CONTRARY DREAMS

Other dream symbols are less easy to understand. Weddings and brides, for instance, are not always the happy omens that one would think, and may warn against a rival in love or of getting into a situation that is best avoided. Dreams about sickness or death can be an indicator of a change for the better.

Such dreams are called "contrary" dreams

because their message is the exact opposite of what one would imagine. Dream interpreters have crystalized their ideas about contrary dreams after years of recording their after-effects.

SHARED DREAMS

Shared dreams occur when two people have an almost identical dream. There may be a meaning to these dreams that links the two dreamers in some way.

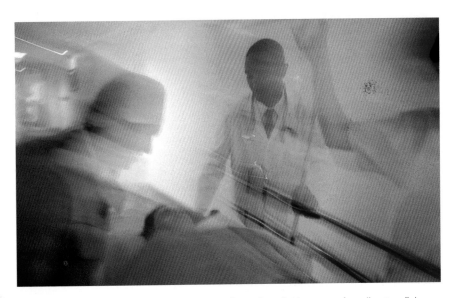

Dreaming of sickness can be a "contrary" dream.

Shared dreams show a telepathic link.

Even when it has been switched off, your computer is only snoozing!

DÉJÀ VU AND THE SPIRITS

Occasionally, a dream appears to be a form of déjà vu that takes the dreamer back to a past life. Whether you believe in reincarnation and interpret it as warning against making the same mistakes again or not, such a dream message will be relevant to something that is going on in your life and should be taken seriously.

Sometimes a sleeping person will dream that a relative who has died visits them and brings them a message. Many people believe that it is easier for the person who is "in spirit" to get through to a loved one while they are asleep and that it may be the departed loved one's way of telling the sleeping person that they are near and keeping watch over them. Such a dream should always be heeded, as it may contain useful advice or a warning to the sleeper.

DREAMS OF WARNING AND ADVICE

A friend told me this story. Many years ago, while she was happily organizing her forthcoming wedding, she dreamed night after night of being slammed in prison and left alone. In her dream, she hung onto the bars of the heavy jail door shouting herself hoarse, but nobody came to her rescue. My friend told her mother about this dream, but she dismissed it as simply revealing her prewedding nerves.

My friend duly got married. The wedding was a great success and she joyfully set off for her honeymoon with her handsome new husband. Within 24 hours, however, this charming young man had turned into a moody, hypercritical monster who criticized her appearance, clothes, and, indeed, everything that she did. He also feigned illness so that she would run around after

DO ANIMALS DREAM?

Nobody knows for sure whether animals dream, but, judging by their R.E.M. activity, one must suppose that they do so.

Some tests have been done on dolphins, who manage to swim about and maintain a level of alertness — even coming up for air – while they are asleep. It appears that half of their brain shuts down, leaving just enough working consciousness to enable them to survive. This phenomenon can be compared to a computer that has been shut down and has even had its electricity supply shut off, but still maintains a certain amount of battery-driven activity.

him. Yet between each bout of critical or unhinged behavior, he once again turned into the sunny, humorous, intelligent, and loving man whom she thought she had married.

Her husband was a classic abuser and, needless to say, the marriage didn't last. My friend eventually met someone else, but she was understandably reluctant to commit herself again. One night, she dreamed that her mother (who had died in the meantime) was telling her to go ahead and trust her new lover because he was a good man. Her mother was right, and my friend now has a decent and loving husband.

So, as you can see, dreams should be taken seriously because they may be giving you an important message that comes from either inside yourself or from a outside spiritual source. Now read on – and have sweet dreams!

Dreams of entrapment or prison should always be taken seriously.

the dream dictionary

The meanings given in this book are intended as a general

guide and that some meanings may differ according to

folklore, tradition, or psychological school.

A

ABANDONMENT

The interpretation of this dream depends upon who or what is being abandoned. If it is you who is being abandoned, this dream may be in response to the fact that someone has left you or let you down. It may be warning you that your love relationship is not all that you think it is and that you might soon find yourself being abandoned. If you dream that you are abandoning a job or a situation, this indicates that you are ready to move on.

ABBESS OR ABBOT

Dreaming of meeting an abbess or nun suggests that you will soon have to submit to some kind of authority figure. If the abbess is friendly, then you have wise friends who will stand by you. Seeing an abbot warns of losses or ill health to come. Spite and malice might be around you soon.

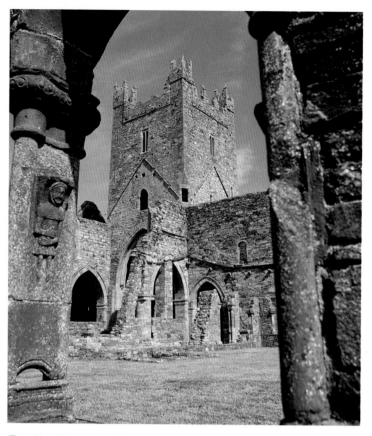

The abbey brings peace for some, disappointment for others.

ABBEY

If the abbey is intact, this suggests that spiritual help and guidance, as well as peace of mind, are on the way. If the abbey is in ruins, then your hopes could be due to fall apart. If a young woman dreams of entering an abbey, she could soon be in trouble for gossiping about others. See also convent, monk.

ABDOMEN

A large, full stomach suggests good times to come and also productivity. An empty or shriveled abdomen means that your friends will let you down and also that you will be short of money for a while.

ABORTION

Dreaming of abortion suggests that your plans will miscarry. It can also foretell a period of poor health.

A

ABUNDANCE

Money and an affluent lifestyle are on the way, but your domestic situation might not be as successful as your financial one. See also affluence, riches.

ABUSE

Whether you dream that you are being abused or are handing out abuse, this warns that you must take care that you do not ride roughshod over others, especially in matters of business.

ACCEPTANCE

To dream that a business proposal has been accepted is a very good omen and hints that a bad spell of trading will soon improve. The same optimistic outlook applies when you dream that a proposal of marriage has been accepted.

ACCIDENT

Although this dream is often simply an acknowledgement that you have worries and woes, it may foretell an actual accident. Perhaps it would be best to avoid traveling for a month following a dream like this.

Accounts dreams mean a good "bottom line."

ACCORDION

Hearing an accordion playing, or dreaming of playing one, indicates future celebrations and parties.

ACCOUNTS

Oddly enough, dreaming of accounts can foretell a happy love affair or marriage. In a business context, if the accounts add up, then all will be well, but if they don't, the dream is warning that the company is running into difficulties.

ACE

In general, an ace indicates success and a windfall, but if your dream shows you which of the four aces it is, it is telling you which sphere of your life it will apply to. Dreaming of the ace of clubs denotes financial security. The ace of diamonds indicates new ventures, a promotion, and sometimes also a letter bringing good news. The ace of hearts means that romance is on the way. The ace of spades signifies that troubles lie ahead and you may have to take things into your own hands in order to solve a problem. See also cards.

Lucky at cards, lucky in love?

Advertisements show that someone wants your attention.

ACORNS

Dreaming of acorns suggests that pleasant times and prosperity are on the way. Picking acorns signifies that hard work will bring success. Acorns can sometimes indicate a legacy. See also oak.

ACROBAT

An acrobat hints of danger while traveling and also warns against being drawn into dangerous schemes by others. Business matters will not be well starred and friends could let you down.

ACTOR, ACTRESS

If you dream of an actor or actress, you may be called upon to play a part rather than simply being yourself. The part played by the actor or actress is important: if they are in a happy role, good times are coming, but if they are acting out a tragedy, you may lose out, in love or in some other way. See also play, theater.

ADDER

Dreaming of an adder indicates that you may marry a rich person, but that this will provoke jealousy among your friends. See also snake, viper.

ADMIRAL

A dream admiral hints at an imminent rise in your status. See also navy.

ADMIRATION

Dreaming of being an object of admiration denotes that you will soon encounter love.

ADULTERY

A dream of adultery may be the result of guilty feelings, but may also stem from a fear of being unfaithful. It may also simply be a harmless fantasy that is better dreamed about than acted upon in waking life. See also bigamy.

ADVANCEMENT

Dreaming of advancement in any form often foretells a promotion at work.

ADVERTISEMENT

If an advertisement features in your dream, it suggests that your circumstances will soon improve. If you are a young woman, it hints that a certain man would like to meet you. In a business context, it denotes a successful advertising and marketing campaign.

Fly away to freedom.

AFFLUENCE

Dreaming of affluence means on the one hand that money may be coming your way, but on the other it warns that you should be good to your parents and family. See also abundance, riches.

AGONY

A dream in which agony features indicates that although business will be fine, there may be trouble ahead in connection with your relationships or within your household. See also pain, torture.

AIR

Whether the air that you dream about is hot, cold, or you have simply noted it, air denotes troubles to come, especially in connection with your job.

AIRPLANE

Travel may be indicated by a dream airplane, or a time of freedom that may soon present itself. See also jet, parachute, propeller.

AISLE

Dreaming of an aisle does not foretell a wedding, but instead indicates being stuck in a situation that you have no control over.

ALBUM

Looking through a photograph album in a dream is a good omen that signifies friendship and love. See also picture.

ALIEN

Dreaming of any type of alien indicates that you will meet new and interesting friends.

ALLEY

If the alley is wide and bathed in sunlight in your dream, the future looks bright. If it is narrow and dark, it warns that you must take care in the future. See also path.

ALLIGATOR, CROCODILE

Beware of people who will walk all over you or take a "bite" out of you if your dream features an alligator.

Affluence should be shared.

Almonds mean prosperity.

ALLOWANCE

Dreaming of being given an allowance by your parents or any other relative indicates happiness ahead. If the allowance is given to you by a questionable person, future problems are denoted.

ALMONDS

All dreams about nuts and seeds signify prosperity and saving for the future. If you are currently unhappy, such dreams promise that it won't be for long.

ALTAR

If you dream of an altar, quarrels in your business or personal life may be indicated. You may need to make an apology.

AMETHYST

An amethyst in a dream signifies peace of mind, contentment, and happiness, that is, unless the amethyst has been lost, in which case broken engagements or relationships are being foretold.

AMMUNITION

Unless you dream of running out of ammunition, which indicates that you will find it hard to finish what you have started, an ammunition dream means that your work will come to a successful end. See also gun.

AMPUTATION

If you dream of an amputated limb, you should beware of losses.

This dream urges you to express your feelings.

A

ANCHOR

Interpreters suggest various meanings for a dream anchor. If you are due to travel, your trip will be successful, but if you prefer to stay put, this will also be the right decision. An anchor may also suggest business worries or a quarrel with a lover, due either to differences of opinion about future choices or issues of freedom.

ANGEL

The meaning of a dream that features an angel depends on the appearance of the angel and whether it gives any advice or a warning. It can mean spiritual guidance and protection, but may also be warning against acting immorally or unkindly toward others in the future. See also heaven.

ANGER

Dreaming of being angry suggests that you really are feeling angry, but are suppressing your feelings either for the sake of peace or because you feel that your anger is unjustified. It suggests that it might be better to be more assertive, to put your foot down, speak out, and risk a quarrel than to swallow your anger and make yourself ill as a result.

ANGLING

See fish, fishing.

ANIMALS

Seeing peaceful animals in a dream suggests success and prosperity. If you have to fight off a fierce animal, this denotes that you will win through.

ANTELOPE

If an antelope features in your dream, it signifies that if you put your mind to something, you will succeed.

ANTS

Traditionally, dreaming of ants denotes that although you will have to work hard, you will be happy with the results of your efforts. However, see page 10 for a more unusual interpretation and be prepared to work hard while keeping an eye on your mother-in-law!

ANVIL

A dream anvil is indicative of success and also denotes that strong bonds will soon be forged.

APPLAUSE

Applause is a contrary dream symbol, because it indicates that rather than being fêted, you could be surrounded by envious or unpleasant people who don't think much of you.

APPLE

The apple is a symbol of love, and also of fertility, especially if the apple is red and has leaves growing close to it. If an apple is growing on a tree in your dream, take note of its position. The most positive message is being sent when it is within reach. If it is too high, your aims may be too ambitious, and if it is rotting on the ground, you may be missing out on something good. See also fruit.

This tempting apple tells of love.

A

The arch is great for professional life, but not for romance.

APRICOTS

An old proverb says that dreaming of apricots means that you are wasting valuable time. See also fruit.

APRON

If an apron features in your dream, it suggests that there will soon be a lot of work to do, also possibly denoting a promotion or increase in status at work.

AQUAMARINE

An aquamarine signifies a happy love life, that is, unless you have lost it, in which case you should beware of losing your lover.

ARAB

If a young woman dreams of meeting an Arab, this suggests that she will soon start dating a quiet man, but that the relationship won't last. Another interpretation that fits a work or business situation is either dealing with exports or traveling on business.

ARCH

As far as your social status and professional life are concerned, dreaming of an arch denotes a rise in status and coming to the attention of people who previously ignored you. It is not such a good sign for romance, however, as it signifies that a lover will let you down, a rival may be on the scene, or that your lover's parents won't accept you. A fallen arch states either that the romance is over or, worse still, that a hasty marriage will land you in a bad situation.

ARCHER

If you dream of an archer, you could soon find yourself in competition with others. Additionally, a person born under the zodiacal sign of Sagittarius may soon become important to you. See also arrow.

ARM

In a dream scenario, an arm signifies unhappiness in a relationship followed by separation and divorce. It may also warn that you are surrounded by deceit and fraud. It may sometimes indicate illness, or even a death, in the family. See also elbow, sleeve.

ARMY

If you see an army in your dream, this suggests that you will soon become involved in a battle. See also battle, marching, soldier, uniform.

An army dream foretells a battle.

A

ARREST

Dreaming of being arrested, or seeing others being arrested, sends a positive message of success and happiness. However, it also warns that you should chose any new friends with care. See also police.

ARROW

A dream arrow may indicate that love is coming your way, although if the arrow has been snapped, a broken love affair is signified. See also archer.

ART, ARTISTS

Dreaming of painting or creating something beautiful signifies that you should not stifle your creativity. You should also guard against false friends. See also gallery, picture.

Cupid's arrow, perhaps?

ASPARAGUS

An asparagus is a male fertility symbol that indicates to the dreamer that a sexy relationship or a pregnancy is imminent. See also vegetables.

A

ASSASSIN

A dream assassin is a clear warning of danger, foretelling either a mugging or similar physical attack on your person or a metaphorical stab in the back by a colleague or false friend. Dreaming of an assault has a related meaning, suggesting that those who work for you could betray you. See also attack.

ASTHMA

If asthma features in your dream, it may indicate either sickness to come or a collapse of your plans. See also bronchitis, illness.

ASYLUM

Dreaming of an asylum warns that you, or someone close to you, will soon run into difficulties. You may be called upon to help a friend.

An asthma dream should be taken seriously.

ATHLETE

A dream athlete suggests that although there are trials ahead of you, you should be successful.

ATLAS

Seeing an atlas in a dream suggests travel in connection with either love or business. See also map.

ATTACK

Dreaming of an attack warns you that you should take no chances over the following month. See also assassin, blows, fighting, rape.

ATTIC

If an attic features in your dream, it suggests that you will achieve your goal. If you accept a new job, you will find it enjoyable. See also house, room.

ATTORNEY, ADVOCATE, LAWYER, OR SOLICITOR

Dreaming of an attorney, advocate, lawyer, or solicitor means that you will get the advice that you need if you ask for it. You may be worrying about legal matters, but these should work out all right in the end. See also bar, lawyer.

AUCTION

If an auction features in your dream, it is a good business omen – especially in relation to farming – that also indicates that there will be no shortage of money in the home. If you dream of not being able to buy or sell something you want, this signifies that you should take care in future business or money dealings and should avoid lending money to others.

AUNT

Dreaming of an aunt suggests that either your actual aunt or another older woman will soon help you. See also uncle.

AUTOMOBILE

An automobile is an amazingly common thing to dream about, and its meaning depends on what is happening in your dream. If the automobile is under control and running smoothly, your life will soon become easy and successful. If the car is careering out of control, whether you are inside it or on the outside, chasing it down the road, you could have more to deal with than you can cope with. It also signifies that you may find yourself among people who are out of control. See also garage, mechanic, taxi, vehicle, wagon, wheel.

The author is saying here "Write that bestseller!"

AUTUMN

See fall.

AUTHOR

If you dream of an author and actually are a writer, take note of what is happening in the dream as it could be prophetic.

The auctioneer brings news about business.

B

BABY

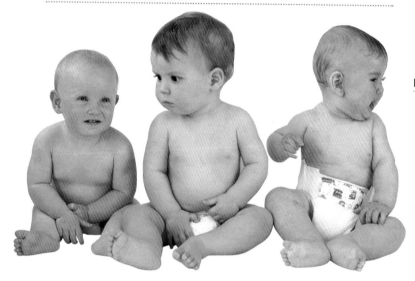

Whatever the baby is doing in the dream – whether it is being born or is dead or dying – it is a sign of good fortune and the start of something new. If the baby is walking unaided, it indicates increasing independence on your part. See also birth, child, children, cradle, daughter, pregnancy.

BACHELOR OR SPINSTER

If a man dreams of being a bachelor, it suggests that he is unsure about becoming more involved in a relationship. When a woman dreams of a bachelor or spinster, this is what she is wishing for.

BACK

Dreaming of a naked back indicates a loss of power and potential sickness. It suggests that lending money or giving advice may be dangerous, especially if it is your own back that you are dreaming about. Whether it is clothed or not, seeing the back of someone else signifies that someone will soon walk away from you.

BACK DOOR

If you are using the back door of your house in your dream, it suggests that changes are on the way. If friends enter your house through the back door, this

could be warning that you should avoid becoming caught up in their schemes. Dreaming of robbers may also be a warning. See also door, doorbell, robber

BACON

Bacon in a dream signifies business losses, the possibility that friends may desert you, or that you may lose something that is important to you. See also pig, meat.

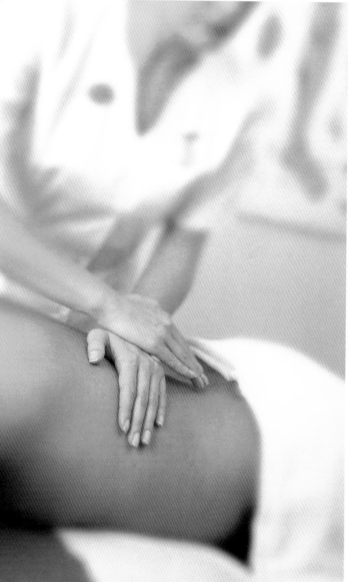

Watch your back!

Bacon dreams denote losses.

BAG

Dreaming of a bag is generally a positive omen that suggests that you will shortly have something good, perhaps money, to put in your bag. It may also denote that you have hidden talents that you will soon be able to release from the bag. Looking into the bag and finding it empty is not such a positive omen, however, as it indicates that you will be disappointed in some way. A handbag may signify that you are feeling a little lost because your identity is being attacked. See also briefcase, sack.

BAGPIPES

Seeing bagpipes in a dream promises some jolly times ahead.

BAILIFF

If you dream that a bailiff is taking your possessions away from you, it is a warning that you should not put your trust in others.

BAKER OR BAKING

Dreaming of a baker or baking is always a good signal because it suggests an end to poverty. It also denotes an improvement in the mental or physical condition of your children. See also bread, cakes, dough, doughnut, flour, oven, yeast.

BALCONY

See gallery.

BALDNESS

If you dream of a bald man, he is warning you not to deal with people who are pressing you to make deals that are to their advantage and not yours. If a man dreams of a bald woman, he could end up with a real vixen for a wife.

BALL

There are two kinds of ball, the one that you play sports with and the one that you attend, and both are good omens in dreams. Dreaming of the type that you play with suggests that opportunities are coming your way, while if you dream of going to a ball, this hints that you will soon be very happy.

The baker brings prosperity and healthy children.

Balloons signify a cheerful dream.

BANQUET

If you dream that you are enjoying yourself at a banquet, prosperity and happy times ahead are suggested. If the banquet is a bit of a flop, however, then misunderstandings and disappointment are indicated.

BAPTISM

A baptismal dream is an important one, and the message within it should be taken seriously. It may indicate that you need to change your ways or lifestyle for the better. If you dream about a specific religious figure, such as John the Baptist, you should reconsider your behavior and way of life.

BALLET

If ballet features in your dream, it may signify that an attack of rheumatism is imminent. Otherwise, it may indicate jealousy, an unfaithful partner, or else business losses.

BALLOONS

Dream balloons tell you not to take anything too seriously for a while.

BANANA

Dreaming of a banana suggests that a relationship is in a state of flux and probably won't work out well in the end.

BANK, BANKNOTE, OR BANKRUPTCY

In a dream, banks, banknotes, and bankruptcy all indicate future money troubles and warn against taking chances in business.

BANNER

If a banner features in your dream, you can take it as a good omen that suggests that you will soon achieve something that you can be proud of. It also indicates that others will think well of you.

BAR

Dreaming of working or drinking in a bar augurs well for friendship and also hints that your children will make you proud of them. Being called to the bar as a barrister denotes that you will soon have a fight on your hands. See also attorney, lawyer.

Bananas spell disappointments.

If you dream of banknotes, check your finances now!

BARBECUE

A dream barbecue warns that friends or relatives may impose themselves on you.

BARBER

If a barber appears in your dream, this indicates that paying attention to detail will result in success. See also hair, razor, scissors.

BAREFOOT

Dreaming of walking barefoot and being dressed in rags warn against becoming embroiled in difficulties or of walking upon dangerous ground. Such dreams signify that poverty and loss may be on the way. See also beggar, feet, shoes, walking.

BARN

In dream interpretation, a barn indicates that you will soon be in a position where you have money put by and plenty to spare. It can also denote marriage to a rich partner or inheriting wealth. If the barn is empty or decrepit, however, the opposite meanings apply.

BASEBALL

A baseball dream hints at fun and games and happy times ahead.

BASKET

If the basket in your dream is full, it represents success and prosperity. If it is empty, however, it indicates that hard times are approaching.

BAT

If a bat features in your dream, take it as a sign that you shouldn't lend any money and should be careful whom you trust.

BATH, BATHING

Dreaming of a bath or bathing is significant and can be interpreted in a number of ways, depending upon the dream circumstances. Generally speaking, bathing in the open air is considered a good omen for love and for life itself, that is, unless you find yourself bathing in a muddy or weed-choked pool. As long as the water is warm and the bath is clean, bathing inside indicates future prosperity. If the bath water is cold, however, losses may be incurred. If other people are around you while you are bathing, take it as a warning that you are vulnerable to attack. Bathing in the sea can be interpreted as washing your troubles away. See also shower, soap, sponge, washing, water.

B

BATTLE

Take note of the circumstances of the battle in your dream. If you were not involved in it, for instance, you may shortly be called upon to act as a peacemaker. If you were involved, take whether you won or lost the battle as an indication of the outcome of a future event. See also army, soldier.

BEANS

Dreaming of beans suggests that sickness is threatening to strike your family, particularly your children, so take special care with hygiene. Eating a bean, especially a dried one, implies that you yourself will soon become sick. Dried beans may also suggest disappointment in business affairs. See also vegetables.

BEAR

If you see a bear in your dream, it indicates that difficulties lie ahead. If the bear attacks you and you overcome it, you should eventually succeed in your quest.

Beards mean success for farmers!

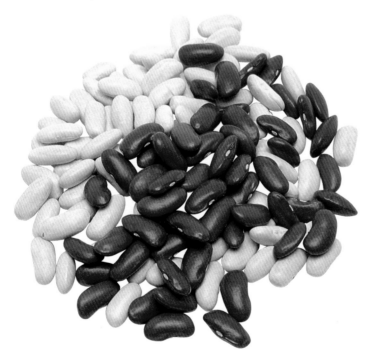

Bean dreams are a health warning.

BEARD

In dreams, beards may sometimes signify unexpected success, the bigger the beard, the better the outcome. Beards may augur well for future prosperity, especially in connection with land or farming, although another interpretation is that someone will oppose you and that there will be a clash of wills. A gray beard often suggests bad luck and quarrels, combing a beard indicates vanity, while having your own beard trimmed warns that someone is trying to undermine you. Some interpreters believe that if you are a woman and dream that you are a bearded man, it could be a reference to a previous life. They advocate that you try to work out what the dream is telling you and to accept the advice or warning given. See also hair.

BED

If dreamers see themselves sleeping or resting in bed, it may mean that they will soon be able to take some time off for a well-deserved rest. In other circumstances, dreaming of a bed can indicate a great new lover. If the bed is unmade, you should take care not to get into any trouble, and if you happen to be ill at the time of the dream, it may be warning you that you will become worse. A mother who dreams that her child wets the bed is probably unconsciously aware that the child is troubled. Dreams of sharing a bed generally augur well for the future, but if a strange bedfellow makes you feel uneasy, it could be telling you something about your love relationship. Animals in the bed denote bad luck, while bedbugs foretell illness and possibly a fatality.

BEEF

If beef features in your dream, it may signify that accidents, bruises, burns, sickness, or other physical ailments may befall you. See also bull, cattle, meat.

BEES

In the dream world, bees indicate success, progress, and prosperity through hard work. A swarm of bees augurs well for your personal and family finances. See also hive, honey, wasps.

BEETLES OR BUGS

If bugs are beetling about in your dream, they are warning of small setbacks and losses. See also vermin.

BEGGAR

Dreaming of a beggar indicates that although you may be in a certain amount of trouble, you should soon receive some much-needed help. See also barefoot.

BEHEADING

There are many interpretations of beheading dreams, some considering them to be bad omens that foretell disaster, such as exile or a death in the family. However, other sources claim that beheading dreams are good omens that signify a liberation from debts, family troubles, sickness, and other unhappy circumstances. See also execution, head.

BELLOWS

If bellows feature in your dream, you may have psychic powers.

BELLS

Dreaming of bells indicates that news will soon come your way. The nature of the news depends upon the dream: if it is a happy dream, for example, the news will be good. See also church.

Bells ring out the good news.

B

BELT

If you dream of a belt, it may be telling you that it is time to tighten your belt and be less extravagant. See also buckle, girdle.

BENCH

If you dream of sitting on a bench, take it as a warning that someone who owes you money may let you down. If you see other people sitting on a bench, a joyous reunion is signified, or perhaps making up with friends after an argument.

BIBLE

In dream symbolism, the Bible promises innocent pleasures and happy times ahead.

BICYCLE

Decision time has arrived if you dream of a bicycle. When making your decision, it is better to act upon your intuition than to depend upon the advice or opinions of others. See also wheel.

BIGAMY

A bigamous dream shows that your mind is muddled and your love life confused. See also adultery.

BINOCULARS

As long as you are using the binoculars for innocent purposes in your dream, they are a positive symbol. If you dream that you are spying on someone, it could indicate that someone will soon spy on you.

BIRDS

Dreaming of birds is common, and the many possible interpretations depend on their type and behavior. High-flying birds denote successful undertakings. If the birds are caged, you may be feeling restricted or trapped. Many birds together may denote law suits,

Binoculars warn you to be on the lookout for spies and snoopers.

B

while dreaming of birds entering a house suggests losses. Hearing birds singing may refer to a wedding or celebration, but crows, blackbirds, and magpies signify funerals. See also buzzards, chickens, cocks, crows, dove, ducks, eagle, eggs, feathers, geese, hawk, jackdaw, magpies, nest, ostrich, owl, parrot, peacock, penguin, pigeon, ravens, sparrow, swan, vulture.

BIRTH

Dreaming of a baby hints at good news for married or attached women, but if the dreamer is a single woman, it may mean that their lover will leave them. See also baby, pregnancy.

BIRTHDAY, BIRTHDAY PRESENTS

In the dream world, birthdays and birthday presents foretell a happy event, a windfall, or an improvement in your working situation.

BISCUITS

See cookies.

BLACKBOARD

If a blackboard features in your dream, it may signify that interesting news is on its way. If you noticed any writing on the board, the news may arrive very shortly. See also school.

BLACKMAIL

Dreaming of blackmail sends a direct warning that you should guard against laying yourself open to this.

BLANKET

Dreams that focus on blankets concern your finances and investments. If you dream of buying blankets, you will lose money, but if you dream of selling them, you will gain it. Torn or dirty blankets augur badly for finances.

Birthdays bring good things in dreams, too.

B

In dreams, blood spells business problems.

BLOOD

Blood is a bad omen in dreams, especially for those in business, dealings with foreigners or foreign places being especially badly starred. It also warns that jealous and malicious people surround you. See also vampire.

BLOSSOMS

Dream blossoms signify prosperity. See also flowers, trees.

BLOWS

If you dream that you are fighting off an aggressor's blows, your career or business should improve. If you dream of being hurt, you should beware of potential danger. See also attack, boxing.

BOAT

In a dream, a boat usually suggests a journey undertaken in connection with love or loved ones. Unless the sea is very stormy, it may indicate married happiness. See also canoe, gondola, lake, oar, propeller, sailing, sailor, yacht.

BOIL, BOILING

Dreaming of boiling liquids warns that your feelings are about to boil over. See also kettle, saucepan.

BOILER

Beware if you dream about a boiler being out of action, as this can warn of losses and disappointments. Even if the boiler is in good condition, sickness and troubles are possibilities.

BOMB

A dream bomb is an unambiguous warning of imminent danger.

Boats signify travel in connection with love.

BOOK

If a book features in your dream, it suggests that you either need to discover certain information or that you will shortly embark upon a course of study. Dreaming of children reading books denotes happy, healthy children and harmonious relationships between the generations in your family. See also bookcase, bookshop, dictionary.

BOOKCASE

If your dream bookcase is full of books, it signifies that you will enjoy your work and will make headway in your career. If it is empty, however, you will find your job irksome. See also book.

Dream of books for healthy children.

BOOKSTORE

A bookstore dream suggests that your head is so crammed with unrealistic ideas that it is interfering with your daily life. See also book.

BOOMERANG

Seeing a boomerang in a dream indicates that something will be revisited on you: the good or bad turns that you did to others, for instance, may now rebound on you.

BOX

If your dream box is full, you may soon receive a windfall, but if it is empty, you may be short of money for a while.

BOXING

Dreaming of boxing warns that secrets must be kept. See also blows.

BRA

If a woman dreams of a bra, it denotes an improvement in her status and social life. If the dreamer is male, the message could be to be careful about whose bra you handle!

BRACELET

If the bracelet in your dream is intact, it symbolizes union and partnership. If it is broken, it foretells the end of a partnership.

BRANDY

A dream in which brandy makes an appearance suggests that although you will attain the social position that you are longing for, your social graces won't be good enough for you to maintain it.

BREAD

Dreaming of bread can signify good luck and prosperity, but may also mean having to work hard to feed children who may return this favor by being stubborn and ungrateful. Loaves sometimes signify a shortage of money and quarrels among family members. See also baker, dough, flour, jam, rye, yeast.

B

BREAKFAST

This is a good dream for those who use their brains in their job. Seeing a hearty breakfast on the table and sharing it with others generally augurs well, although it may indicate that a few changes are on the way. Eating alone warns that your enemies may get the better of you.

BRIBE

Bribe dreams offer clear warnings about the consequences of being caught giving or receiving bribes.

BRIDE, BRIDEGROOM, BRIDESMAID

A wedding dream means the opposite of what you might think. At best, it can foretell a legacy, but is more likely to indicate disappointment in love. See also confetti, wedding.

A briefcase signifies a "contrary" dream.

BRIDGE

If the bridge is in one piece in your dream and you can, or do, cross it safely, this signifies the end of a troubled period. If the bridge is broken, or you have an accident while crossing it, you should consider your future path because it is not secure. If you pass under a bridge, your life is reasonably stable, but still not very secure. See also gangway.

BRIEFCASE

Briefcase dreams are contrary dreams in that a full briefcase warns that you have much to do and that you must avoid losses in business. An empty briefcase hints that your work situation will improve and that money is coming. See also bag.

BROADCAST

If you dream of listening to a broadcast, success is on its way. Dreaming of being on the radio or television advises you to persevere with your work and plans.

BRONCHITIS

Perhaps unsurprisingly, a bronchitis dream foretells sickness and disappointments. See also asthma, illness.

BROOM

Dreaming of a broom suggests that sweeping changes are imminent. See also brush, sweeping.

BROTHERS

If the brothers in your dream are doing well, all is well with you. If, on the other hand, they are poor or unhappy, you may not be happy yourself in the near future. See also sisters.

BRUSH

Dreaming of a variety of brushes suggests that you will soon be doing a job that involves a number of tasks. A clothes brush promises success through hard work. Dreaming of brushing your hair signifies misfortune and mismanagement. See also broom.

BUBBLES

Dream bubbles denote fun and frivolity.

BUCKLE

Seeing a fastened buckle in a dream indicates a happy family life, while one that is unfastened represents family troubles and arguments. If you find yourself doing up a buckle in your dream, you should pay attention to your business affairs. See also belt, girdle.

Bubbles spell fun.

BUGLE

A dream bugle trumpets the news that joyous times are on their way.

BUILDING

If a building features in your dream, it may foretell a beneficial change in your circumstances and building for the future.

BULL

Dreaming of a bull may prophesy that someone born under the zodiacal sign of Taurus will shortly become important to you. Alternatively, someone close to you may behave obstinately. See also beef, cattle.

BULLDOG

If the dream dog is friendly, it is likely that you will be quite successful in the future. If it is fierce, it is warning you not to break the law. See also dog, kennel.

BURDEN

Carrying a burden in your dream denotes that you will be weighed down by cares and worries. Putting down a burden indicates a great improvement in your circumstances. See also income tax.

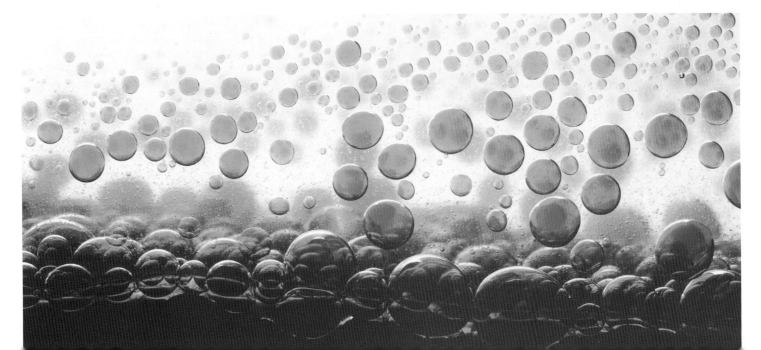

B

BURGLAR

See back door, robber.

BURIAL

Oddly enough, a burial dream is an indication of a happy marriage and possibly also of a windfall. If you dream of a relative or friend being buried, it may signify that they are leaving your circle to travel to or live somewhere else. See also cemetery, coffin, grave.

BURNS

In the dream world, burns denote success and an end to troubles, future good fortune, and fast friends.

BUS

Dreaming of waiting for a bus signifies temporary setbacks, while catching the bus hints that you will get your heart's desire. An accident involving a bus represents financial setbacks.

BUTCHER

Seeing a butcher kill an animal in a dream suggests that sickness will befall you or your family. Watching a butcher cutting up meat may warn that someone will give you a bad character reference. You should also be careful about what you put in writing. See also meat.

BUTTER

If butter features in your dream, it may symbolize good health and a successful outcome to your plans. Selling butter can be equated with small gains or windfalls.

BUTTERFLY

In the dream world, a butterfly signifies prosperity and success. If the dreamer is a young woman, it may indicate a wonderful future lover. A number of butterflies represents the arrival of news from friends.

Catching a bus is better than waiting for one.

BUTTONS

To a young woman, dreaming of buttons promises a pleasant and wealthy husband, while to a young man it signifies a successful career.

BUZZARD

Dream buzzards warn of scandal, loss, arguments, and gossip. See also birds.

Dream buttons bring a happy marriage.

Cages infer issues of entrapment and escape.

CABIN

If you dream of a ship's cabin, you can be almost sure that somebody will try to hurt you and that there could even be legal complications.

CAGE

The interpretation of a dream cage depends on its circumstances. For instance, if you dream of being in a cage, you are being warned to guard against getting yourself into a situation that you can't get out of. If you, or something or someone else, escapes from a cage, you will either avoid becoming trapped or will find a way out of a present predicament. If you leave a cage door open and something that shouldn't escape does, you could be on the point of losing your lover or someone or something else precious to you through carelessness and neglect.

CAKES

If cakes feature in your dream, they signify happy times and celebrations to come. See also doughnuts, flour.

CALENDAR

Dreaming of a calendar may be a reminder that time is running out or that an important date is approaching.

CAMEL

In the dream world, a camel may indicate that you are carrying too many burdens.

CAMERA

Dreaming of a camera foretells disappointment, a disastrous change of job, or even a house move to a place where you are not comfortable. See also films.

CAMP

If you dream of camping out, your life is about to change and you may have to take an important and tiring journey, while seeing others in a camp means that they are going away. If a young woman has a camping dream, she is unsure about committing to a relationship, but if she dreams of visiting a military camp, the opposite applies, and she will try to settle down with the first man who comes her way. See also tent.

Calendars warn that time is running out.

C

CAMPAIGN

Dreaming of any kind of campaign, be it political, religious, or business, denotes that you will have to struggle to get your point of view across to others.

CANAL

A canal dream refers to your future security. You will be secure if the canal is full, but if it is empty, you will not. See also drowning, river.

CANCER

Oddly enough, if you dream of having cancer, this is a hint that you will soon recover from an illness.

CANDLE

In the dream world, a lit candle denotes strength of purpose and good fortune. An unlit candle warns that you may miss out on an opportunity, however. See also flame.

CANDY

Good news or love are signified by dream candy. See also chocolate, fudge, mint.

CANNIBALS

Seeing cannibals in your dream indicates that you should avoid destructive people and should try not to be spiteful or negative yourself.

CANNON

If you dream of a cannon, a fight is looming in which there is a real danger of defeat. See also battle.

CANOE

A dream canoe signifies that you will not be able to count on anybody helping you with your financial problems and that you will need to be self-reliant. See also boat.

CANYON

Dreaming of a canyon is often a warning that you will soon need to be tactful.

CAP

If a cap features in your dream, it indicates celebration and an increase in money. See also clothes, hat.

CAPTAIN

If a young woman dreams of meeting a captain, this may foretell that she will marry a serving officer.

Candles indicate good fortune.

CAR

See automobile.

CARDS

Dreaming that you are happily playing cards means that you will shortly fall in love and marry. Being cheated indicates that there is treachery and jealousy around you. If you dream that your lover is playing cards, it is wise to question his or her intentions.

If you see a particular card in your dream, remember that each suit is associated with a different matter: diamonds with money, hearts with love, clubs with business, and spades with troubles. Aces signify hopeful beginnings and fresh opportunities – even the significance of the ace of spades is positive, because it indicates that you will soon have the power to put things right that are presently wrong.

The court cards send even more specific messages, as follows.

King of diamonds: guard against being hurt by a powerful older man.

King of clubs: a helpful friend.

King of hearts: a faithful lover.

King of spades: opposition to your plans and ambitions.

Queen of diamonds: good news concerning money and property.

Queen of clubs: business is fine, but your love life may

Read the card in your dream to discover its meaning.

be in a mess.

Queen of hearts: romance, joy, and happy news.

Queen of spades: a secret will be revealed.

Jack of diamonds: a useful gift, small windfall, or inheritance.

Jack of clubs: deceit could cause you business losses.

Jack of hearts: a new romance.

Jack of spades: either a rival or opposition to something that is important to you.

See also ace, gambling, king, queen, tarot.

CARGO

If cargo features in your dream, it may promise either a pleasant journey or a small increase in your income. If the cargo is dropped over the side of a ship or falls from a truck, however, you may soon lose some money.

CARNIVAL

In the dream world, a carnival denotes pleasure, fun, or vacations.

Canyons advise that tact will soon be needed.

C

CARPENTER

A carpenter is a very positive symbol that signifies that whatever it is you want, be it at work or in your love or social life, should soon come your way.

CARPETS

Dream interpreters associate carpets with profit and helpful, wealthy friends. Dreaming of selling carpets is more auspicious than dreaming of buying them. If a young woman dreams of carpets, it hints that she will have a wonderful marriage and a lovely home. See also mat.

CARROTS

Dreaming of carrots may signify that you will inherit money or that some forgotten or "buried" cash will soon turn up. See also vegetables.

Carrots indicate buried treasure.

CASTLE

If the dream castle is in good condition, it augurs well for a nice home and future prosperity. If the castle is in ruins, however, your life will be hard.

CAT

Dreaming of a cat denotes different things, depending on the type of cat and what happens in the dream. Most older sources suggest that dreaming of a cat means that you are likely to be robbed or mugged or that a trusted friend will turn out to be treacherous (and even more so if the cat is screaming or mewing). If the cat is thin and dirty, it warns of bad luck, that is, unless you manage to chase it away. Only if the cat is sitting quietly and washing itself is any good luck indicated. See also kitten.

CATERPILLAR

Seeing a caterpillar in your dream denotes that you should watch out for deceitful people.

CATHEDRAL

In dream interpretation, a cathedral warns against envy and jealousy. See also church, organ, pilgrim.

CATTLE

Dreaming of cattle or cows suggests wealth and prosperity if they are fat or have full udders, but hard times if they are lean. Watching calves grazing peacefully denotes festivities, celebrations, and an improvement in your finances. Vicious-looking cattle signify enemies, and scrawny ones, disgrace. If you are driving the cattle, you will have to work hard, while if they are stampeding, you will have to use all of your strength to cope with a situation. If a young woman dreams of cattle, this indicates a fantastic lover. See also beef, bull, milk, oxen.

CAULIFLOWER

If you dream of eating cauliflower, you may soon be reprimanded for not doing your job properly. If a young woman sees cauliflower growing in a garden, it is likely that she will choose her husband to please her parents rather than herself. See also vegetables.

Cattle bring wealth, celebrations, and a wonderful new lover.

CAVE

In dream interpretation, a cave is a warning that you should beware of falling in love with the wrong type of person. It may also mean that your health is in danger.

Cauliflowers advise you to examine your motives.

CEMETERY

Dreams of cemeteries are very common. They are considered to be an indication of recovery from illness or a bad situation. See also burial, coffin, grave, yew tree.

CHAINS

Dreaming that you are chained up is a clear warning that you should think carefully about what you are getting yourself into. If you dream of breaking out of chains, you are already aware of this potential hazard and will soon break free from it.

Chains warn against becoming trapped.

C

Champagne dreams say that mother knows best!

CHAIR

Seeing a chair in your dream signifies news of an absent friend or loved one. In the sense of a "chair" of a committee, it indicates a promotion or rise in status. If you fall off a chair, you may either be in danger of losing your job or may need a rest. See also committee, furniture, table.

CHAMPAGNE

I love this one! If a young woman dreams that she is drinking champagne, she will soon become involved with a worthless man, despite the fact that her parents will warn her about him. See also cork.

CHAMPION

Dreaming of being a champion indicates that you will attract friends through your pleasant nature.

CHARIOT

If you dream of riding in a chariot, it indicates that good opportunities are on the way and that you should take advantage of them. Falling from a chariot, or seeing others fall from one, suggests that you will fall from grace. See also wagon.

CHARITY

Dreaming of giving money to charity suggests that you will be facing hard times in the near future.

CHEESE

If you dream of cheese, don't act in haste and be careful whom you trust.

CHERRIES

Dream cherries hint that you will soon become popular. See also fruit.

CHESS

A chess dream warns that business and money matters will demand your attention and that you will have to be clever to avoid getting into difficulties.

A game of chess warns you to make the right moves.

CHEST

Dreaming of a chest full of goods or a treasure chest signals future prosperity.

CHICKENS

Dream chickens warn against selfishness and losses incurred through stupidity. See also birds, cocks, hens.

CHILD, CHILDREN

Generally speaking, dreaming of children augurs well, especially where money and business are concerned. If the children are happy or are studying or playing quietly, it is an even better omen, but if you are worried about their health or behavior, it may indicate that all is not well with the children in your family. Good friends may also be indicated by a dream about children. See also baby, daughter, girl, orphan, twins.

CHIMNEY

If a chimney features in your dream, it is not a positive sign because it suggests that bad news or events are around the corner. There may, for example, be trouble in connection with love or business in the near future. See also fireplace.

CHINAWARE

Dreaming of chinaware suggests prosperity and a lovely home.

CHINESE PEOPLE

If you dream of Chinese people, you may soon find a way of solving your problems.

CHIPS

In dream symbolism, wood chips represent petty annoyances, while eating chips or fries foretells enjoyable meals with friends and family.

CHOCOLATE

Dreaming of chocolate indicates that you will be able to look after your family and that celebrations, good friends, and a satisfying job await you. See also candy, fudge.

CHOIR

If a young woman dreams of singing in a choir, her lover may soon be paying attention to another woman. For other dreamers, however, a choir indicates cheerful times.

CHRISTMAS

Dreaming of Christmas denotes happy times with family and friends.

CHRYSANTHEMUMS

Generally speaking, dreaming of chrysanthemums is a sign of love and affection, but white flowers mean that a lover may leave you. See also flowers.

C

It's better to dream of being outside a church than inside it.

CHURCH

If you dream that you are outside a church, all will be well, but if you dream that you are inside it, expect trouble. See also bells, cathedral, mass, organ.

CIRCLE

Dream analysts suggest that a circle warns of dangerous liaisons.

CITY

Visiting a strange city in your dreams indicates that circumstances will force you to move house. See also village.

CLAIRVOYANT

Dreaming of being a clairvoyant, or of seeing one, suggests future changes that will not make you happy. See also gypsy.

CLARET, PUNCH

If you dream that you are drinking claret or punch, it signifies that you will make new friends who will think the world of you.

CLOAK

A cloak symbolizes protection from harm.

City dreams indicate a move of house.

C

CLOTHES

If you dream of clothes, take note of their condition and the dream circumstances. If the clothes look respectable, you may be lacking the necessities of life, and if you are also young, you may be disappointed and let down. If the clothes are ragged, they send a real warning of losses to come. Ill-fitting clothes suggest that your love life is difficult, while being unhappy with your outfit denotes rivals in love. If a wife dreams of wearing her husband's clothes, it may indicate that she will be widowed. Admiring other people's clothes warns that you may soon feel envious of others, while wearing a veil signifies that your relationships with others will be difficult. Seeing very old, or very young, people's clothes hints that you will be asked to do something you don't fancy.

The color of the clothing is also significant. White clothes represent sickness and sadness, unless children are wearing white, in which case life will be fairly pleasant. Black clothing denotes quarrels and disappointments. Yellow garments indicate financial improvement and celebration, while blue ones hint at success in your career and good friends. Red clothes signify that you will evade harm and enemies by getting yourself out of trouble in time. Green garments symbolize prosperity and happiness, while multicolored clothes indicate that the pace of life is speeding up and that a mixture of good and bad changes are on the way. See also cap, cloak, coat, fur, gloves, hat, lace, nakedness, rags, shirt, shoes, sleeve, silk, tailor, undressing, velvet, vest.

CLOUDS

Clouds symbolize worry, but if the clouds are scudding away, the worry will pass. See also sky.

CLOVER

Seeing clover in your dream is a lucky all-round omen signifying health, wealth, and a happy marriage.

COAL MINE

If you are working in a coal mine in your dream, this suggests a setback of some kind, although investing in one indicates that your speculation will pay off. Some older traditions assert that when a young woman dreams of mining coal, she will marry a dentist or a real estate agent. See also mine, pit, quarry.

COAT

Dreaming of wearing a new coat suggests that you will write something that will be a success. If the coat is dirty or torn, your losses will continue, while losing a coat denotes having to rebuild following losses. Wearing someone else's coat suggests that you will ask a friend to stand by you and that they will. See also cloak, clothing, fur.

Passing clouds mean passing worries.

It's best to hear a cock crowing at daybreak in your dream.

COCKS

Hearing a dream cock crowing in the morning indicates an early marriage and living in the lap of luxury; hearing one crowing at night, however, signifies the reverse. Cockfights warn of family quarrels. See also chickens, hens.

COFFIN OR CASKET

If a coffin features in your dream, it warns of losses and possibly even of death. See also burial, cemetery.

COFFEE, COFFEE MILL, COFFEE SHOP

Drinking coffee in a dream suggests that other people won't care for your choice of lover. If you are married, expect frequent quarrels. Selling coffee indicates business losses, while seeing, handling, or roasting coffee denotes mixed fortunes in both your love and family life. Ground coffee foretells a hard time and possibly also the horror of attracting the attention of a real creep. A coffee mill warns of danger, and dreaming of a coffee shop specifically tells you to beware of taking up with bad company, plotting against others, or being the victim of others' plots. See also tea, teapot, teacups.

COLLEGE

In dream symbolism, a college signifies advancement or promotion. See also professor, school.

COMET

Seeing a comet in your dream signifies future trials and tribulations. See also meteor, shooting star.

COMMITTEE

Dreaming of being on a committee denotes that you will be given boring or tiresome jobs to do. See also chair.

COMPASS

The appearance of a compass in a dream suggests that you may need to think about your future direction in life.

COMPUTER

Although the interpretation of a dream computer could hardly be drawn from any source of ancient wisdom, dreaming of using the tools of one's trade, writing letters, and doing accounts are all considered to be good dreams that foretell much work to be done and career advancement. See also desk, files, filing cabinet, office.

CONCERT

Dreaming of attending a concert denotes pleasure and celebrations to come. See also opera, orchestra, play.

CONFETTI

If you dream of confetti, this is a hint that a secret may be revealed. See also bride, bridegroom, bridesmaid, wedding.

CONJURER

In dream symbolism, a conjurer denotes a financial setback. See also juggler, magic.

CONSPIRACY

Dreaming of becoming involved in a conspiracy is a straightforward warning that you should beware of just that.

CONVENT

Refuge or safety is indicated by dreaming of a convent. See also abbess, abbey.

CONVICT

Seeing a convict in your dream may foretell disaster, bad news, worry, and an unwise choice of lover. See also prison.

COOKIES

Dream cookies may warn of future stomach trouble.

COOKING

In dream symbolism, cooking is equated with hard work that is well worth the effort, as well with as good times enjoyed with friends and family. See also kitchen, oven.

CORAL

If you dream of red coral, it signifies enduring friendship, although white coral warns that your lover may be unfaithful.

CORK

Dreaming of pulling a cork from a bottle denotes prosperity. If a young woman dreams of pulling a cork from a bottle of champagne, she will have a handsome and attentive lover who will lavish money and affection on her, but is unlikely to stay around for long. Dreaming of inserting corks into bottles signifies that you are well organized and systematic. See also champagne.

CORN

Whether the dream corn is wheat or sweetcorn, and whether it is growing, being harvested, or in any other healthy state, it indicates prosperity and success. If the corn is withered, however, failure is likely to ensue. See also field, harvest, mill, rye.

Healthy corn means a healthy bank balance.

C

CORONATION

Seeing a coronation in your dream hints at wealthy and influential friends. See also crown, emperor, king, queen.

CORPSE

Whether you see a human or an animal corpse in your dream, bad news is signified.

COSMETICS

If cosmetics feature in your dream, they suggest an improvement in your status and social life.

COTTAGE

Seeing a dream cottage means that you either have a mature personality or that you are getting ready to leave a job, be it for new one or for retirement. See also village.

COUNTING

To count money in your dreams is a good omen signifying future prosperity. Counting anything else, however, suggests that you have probably got too much to do and that you should ask other people for help.

Counting in dreams signifies that you will soon have money to count on.

COWS

See cattle.

CRAB

If you dream of a crab, take care that you don't break the law or else you will probably be caught. Alternatively, a person born under the zodiacal sign of Cancer may become important to you in the future. See also lobster.

CRADLE

Dreaming of a cradle indicates prosperity, but if you see yourself rocking a cradle, it denote illness or problems that result from gossiping. See also baby.

CREDIT OR CREDIT CARDS

In dream symbolism, credit or credit cards warn against getting into debt.

CREW

Dreaming of being a member of a ship's crew tells you that you should beware of losing what you have gained. See also sailing, sailor, ship.

CROCODILE

See alligator.

CROSS

Crosses usually signify happy relationships and marriages, and if the cross is a wooden one, this interpretation still applies, although the married couple will be short of money.

CROSSROADS

Dreaming of crossroads hints that decision time is approaching. See also parting, signpost.

Crowds denote happiness and success.

CROWD

Being part of a crowd or seeing one in a dream augurs well for friendship, parties, happy times, and also success in your job or business. If the crowd is restless, however, it could indicate family troubles.

CROWN

Dreaming of a crown denotes both an improvement in your circumstances and travel. Wearing a crown is not such a good omen, however, as it hints that you may suffer financial or other losses. Dreaming of crowning someone else indicates that you are a good person. See also coronation, emperor, king, queen.

CROWS

Be careful in any property dealings if you dream of crows. Crows, magpies, and ravens are also traditionally said to appear in a dream before you hear of a death. See also birds.

CRUTCHES

If crutches feature in your dream, it is likely that you are going through a struggle. If you dream of throwing the crutches away, things will probably improve.

CUCUMBER

Dreaming of a cucumber denotes a pleasant change or recovery from illness.

CUP

A full cup denotes prosperity in dream symbolism, but an empty one signifies losses. See also glass, teapot, teacups.

CUPBOARD OR CLOSET

In dream interpretation, a cupboard is an indication of plenty, that is, as long as it is clean and full. If it is empty or dirty, however, it foretells hard times.

CURTAIN

If someone or something is hiding behind a curtain in your dream, you can be fairly sure that something is going on behind your back.

You may be struggling to get back on your feet if you dream of crutches.

D

DAFFODILS

If you see daffodils in your dream, spring will be a good time for you. See also flowers.

DAGGER

Danger and treachery are around you if a dagger features in your dream. Someone may metaphorically stab you in the back. See also knife, sword.

DAISY

If you dream of daisies in spring or summer, you can expect love and good fortune. If you dream of them in the fall or winter, however, you must beware of giving your trust to strangers. See also flowers.

DANCE

A dream dance hints that you will ignore chores and will instead spend your time making love.

DANGER

Dreams of being in a dangerous situation are very common and warn of hazards to come.

DAUGHTER

If you are hoping to have a child and you dream that you have a daughter, you will probably have a son. See also baby, child, children, girl.

DEAD PEOPLE

Dreaming of family members who have died is common. If you receive a message during such a dream, take it seriously, as it probably gives advice or a warning. See also obituary.

DEATH

Dreams of death and dying are common and usually signify that a phase of your life is coming to an end and that a new one is starting. See also killing, obituary, skeleton, skull, will.

DEER

If the dream deer is grazing happily, it suggests good future friendships. If you kill a deer in your dream, you may inherit money, but will also make enemies. See also stag.

DENTIST

Dreaming of a dentist often means that it is time to book an appointment with one. See also teeth.

DESERT

In dream analysis, a desert signifies that life may be empty for a while.

A desert signifies a temporary phase of emptiness and boredom.

A dial warns against lending money.

D

DESK

If you can't get into the desk or open its drawers in your dream, you may suffer a disappointment. If you can access it, you may soon make some good friends. See also computer, files, filing cabinet, office.

DETECTIVE

If you have done nothing wrong, dreaming of a detective denotes that your status is increasing. If you have something to be ashamed about, it will probably rebound on you.

DEVIL

Dreaming of the devil warns you to beware of doing evil deeds. See also hell.

DIAL

Dials on phones, clocks, or watches represent money matters in dream symbolism, and specifically warn of future losses. It would be best not to lend money or to spend it on unnecessary things.

DIAMONDS

Generally speaking, dreaming of diamonds augurs well for your happiness and can also denote wealth, that is, unless the diamonds are being worn by someone else. See also gems.

DICTIONARY

Dream dictionaries indicate arguments with friends or losing friends. See also book.

DIGGING

If digging features in your dream, it is likely that life will be a uphill affair; that is, unless your digging turns up something worthwhile. Filling in a hole means that although you are making a major effort, you won't succeed. See also plow.

DINNER

Dreaming of a dinner party is a good omen, but dining alone suggests that you will soon be living alone. Dining with a lover foretells a future quarrel.

DIPLOMA

A dream diploma may represent recognition of past efforts, but can also warn you not to become vain and egotistical.

DIRECTOR

Dreaming of being given a place on the board hints that your career and status are set to improve. If you are thrown off the board, however, the opposite is the case.

D

DITCH

If you see a ditch in your dream, be careful not to fall into a trap or to become involved in something that you won't be able to extricate yourself from later. See also pit.

DIVORCE

Dreaming of divorce warns of troubles in your relationship.

DOCKS

If docks feature in your dream, take care when traveling. See also harbor, quay, ship.

DOCTOR

Dreaming of a doctor is a good omen for health and healing. It also denotes that disputes will soon be settled. In addition, although you may have financial problems, these should soon pass. See also hospital, illness, medicine, nurse, operation, surgeon.

A domino represents strategy and tactics.

DOG

Dreaming of a dog has any number of interpretations, depending upon the nature of the dog and on what it is doing. Dogs often indicate friendships, so an appealing one hints at gain and good friends, while a vicious dog indicates friends who will turn on you. See also bulldog, kennel, puppy, whistle.

DOLL

Dream dolls suggest a happy domestic life and a busier social life.

DOLLAR

If a dollar features in your dream, a monetary increase may be imminent. See also money.

DOMINO

You would be advised to plan your future tactics carefully if you see a dream domino.

DONKEY

In dream symbolism, the most positive interpretation of dreaming of a donkey is riding a white donkey, which suggests that you will soon take a journey that may result in fun or money. Otherwise, dreaming of a donkey may foretell that you will do bad things that will later rebound on you.

Dreaming of a doctor indicates a healthy outlook.

D

DOOR, DOORBELL

If you see a door in your dream, or a doorbell is being rung, new opportunities may be opening up for you. See also back door, gate, key, mat, window.

DOUGH

In dream interpretation, dough is equated with health and prosperity. See also baker, baking, bread, cakes, flour, yeast.

DOUGHNUTS

Dream doughnuts hint at an unexpected trip. See also baker, baking, cakes, flour.

DOVE

Happiness in love, as well as peace, is signified by dreaming of a dove. See also birds.

DRAGON

Some dream analysts assert that a dragon represents a frightening person who is hard to overcome, but others regard it as being a lucky symbol. See also monster.

DROWNING

If you dream of drowning in a river, expect troubles to come very soon, while if you dream of drowning in the sea, the troubles will come later rather than sooner. See also flood, river, swimming, water.

DRUGS

Dreaming of being drugged may signify that there is jealousy around you. Taking medicine to cure an ailment indicates an increase in future prosperity. Taking drugs for fun, or selling or buying them, is a bad omen, as it suggests that thieves and other dishonest people surround you. See also medicine, opium, syringe.

DRUNKENNESS

If you dream of being drunk, this often warns that you will either be given the sack or will be caught out doing wrong. The exception is when dreaming of drinking wine, which is a good omen for both sex and business matters.

DUCKS

Dream ducks hint that good news is on its way and foretell a bright future for your home and family life, as well as your prosperity and business. See also birds.

DUNGEON

If a dungeon features in your dream, it warns that those around you may be in danger.

DYNAMITE

Dreaming of dynamite suggests that a sudden change is on its way.

Dream ducks bring good news.

E

If you dream of an eagle, you will soon become a high-flyer.

EAGLE

If the eagle is flying high in your dream, your hopes should be flying equally high. Dreaming of an eagle is considered to be especially lucky for those in business and also for soldiers. If the eagle is wounded or threatens you, difficulties are indicated. See also birds.

EARRINGS

If the dream earrings are intact, they signify a new lover, but if they are broken, it is possible that an existing lover will leave. See also jewelry.

EARTH

Dreams of soil, or of anything that grows in it, often tell you that you need to be down to earth. Perhaps there are too many things going on in your life. If so, you need to focus on the essentials and ignore the rest.

EARTHQUAKE

Interpretations of earthquake dreams are ancient, but the message is still very modern, warning as they do that your house may be in danger from fire, flood, a tornado, or some other natural disaster, including an earthquake. They may even foretell that a government decision could make life difficult for you.

ECHO

If your own voice is echoing in your dream, expect weird experiences in the future. If you hear someone else's voice echoing, it indicates that you will soon hear news that will have a positive effect on those around you.

ECLIPSE

Dreaming of an eclipse of the moon denotes trouble concerning a mother figure. See also moon.

EELS

If live eels feature in your dream, they suggest that you can overcome your problems if you make the effort. Dead eels augur well for love or money. See also fish, snake.

Lunar dreams, including of eclipses, refer to mother figures.

E

EGGS

In dream symbolism, eggs indicate wealth, such as a nest egg. Eating eggs signifies that you will avoid trouble, but buying and selling eggs may foretell a violent family quarrel. See also birds, nest, pancake, yolk.

ELBOW

If you are elbowing your way through a crowd in a dream, this suggests that you will do better than those around you. A pain in the elbow signifies unexpected opposition, while a broken elbow warns of business losses. See also arm.

ELEPHANT

Elephant dreams are wonderful dreams to have because they indicate prosperity. If you feed the elephant in your dream, this augurs even better for your financial position.

Eggs signify both wealth and quarrels.

ELF, FAIRY

Seeing an elf or fairy in your dream suggests that the "little people" are looking after you.

ELOPEMENT

Dreaming of elopement denotes disappointment in love or your general fortune.

EMBROIDERY

If you are doing the embroidery in your dream, contentment is signaled, but if someone else is embroidering, beware of undeclared enemies. See also knitting, needle, sewing, yarn.

EMERALD

A dream emerald could indicate a rival in love on the one hand, but inheriting property on the other. See also gems, jewelry.

EMPEROR

In dream analysis, an emperor promises success and travel. See also coronation, crown, king, queen.

ENGAGEMENT RING

If an engagement ring features in your dream, a wedding could well be on the way. See also jewelry.

ENGINE

Dreaming of an engine is a contrary dream, because if the engine is working well, your career will take a downturn. If the engine is broken or rusty, however, expect promotion and recognition at work.

ENVELOPE

If the dream envelope is open, future news should be good, but if it is closed, something unpleasant could soon be revealed. See also letter, mailman.

E

If you dream of exercise, you will soon need to work hard.

ESCALATOR

Dreaming of standing on an escalator that is moving upward denotes an improvement in your position, but if it is moving downward, there may be a few setbacks in store. See also ladder, path, stairs.

ESCAPE

Dreaming of escaping from a situation is common, and denotes that you will soon be able to escape from a situation that you are fed up with.

EXAMINATION

The meaning of an examination dream depends on how well you cope with the exam. If you passed it easily, your situation should improve and life will be easy for a while. If you struggled and then failed it, however, life may become quite difficult.

EXECUTION

If you dream of seeing an execution, it is likely that you will experience problems due to someone else's carelessness. If it is you who are executed, however, you may soon have money to spare. See also beheading, gallows.

EXERCISE

Dreaming of taking exercise suggests that you will soon have a hard task to perform. See also football, golf.

EXILE

If exile features in your dream, beware of losing something or someone valuable to you.

EYEBROWS

Dreaming of someone with heavy eyebrows is said to promise success, while thin brows denote disappointment. If you dream that your own eyebrows fall off, your lover may not be faithful to you.

EYES

There are many interpretations for every kind of dream that involves eyes, none of them positive, with matters relating to children and the family being especially badly starred. In addition, a rival could run off with your lover, a business could fail, you may lose your job, or may simply do something really stupid. See also faces, nose, squint.

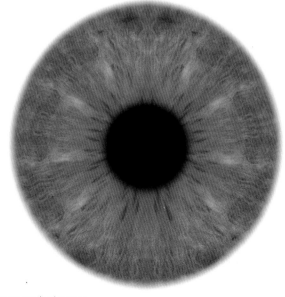

Eye dreams are bad omens.

Dreaming of the fall brings love and money.

F

FACES

You should analyze the looks on the faces that you see your dreams as they reveal what others think of you. If you dream of your own face, a divorce may be on the cards. See also eyes, nose, pimples.

FACTORY

If the factory is busy in your dream, this is a good indication for business, but if it is idle, things may not go so well.

FALL

Fall is the time of year when the fruits of the earth are harvested, so dreaming of this season usually hints that love and money are in the offing. It may also indicate that time is running out, however.

FALLING

Dreams of falling are extremely common and denote insecurity of some kind. They may be warning you that your status will drop or that you may lose your job. See also precipice.

FAME

Dreaming of being famous yourself is not very significant, but dreaming of famous people suggests that your status will rise.

FAMILY

As long your family is happy in your dream, a positive message is being sent, but sickness or unhappiness among family members may otherwise be denoted.

FAN

Dreaming of a fan hints at pleasant news and good friends. If the fan drops, however, your lover could be interested in someone else.

FARMING, FARMERS

Farming dreams indicate that your work is productive. An old source of dream interpretations suggests that dreaming of a farmer means that you will marry one. See also field, plow.

FAT

Dreaming of being fat is a good omen for love, although it also warns that you should watch your health.

FATHER, FATHER-IN-LAW

If a father or father-in-law features in your dream, you may need advice from a father figure. Depending on the dream, it may also foretell family happiness or strife. See also mother, mother-in-law, parents.

Falling dreams are an indication of insecurity.

F

Filing dreams advise you to keep better records.

FAUCET

If you see a faucet or tap in your dream, money may be on its way to you. See also water.

FEATHER

Dream feathers denote small problems that can easily be solved. See also birds.

FEET

Dreaming of feet generally warns you to keep your feet on the ground. If you see feet walking, this suggests that you need to get up and go somewhere or perhaps move away from something or toward something new. Aching feet indicate family troubles, while stockinged feet denote mysteries and secrets. Dirty or cold feet augur badly for love. Large feet signify good health and small ones setbacks. Although burning feet are supposed to symbolize jealousy, they are often a symptom of diabetes, so it would be wise to investigate this possibility. See also barefoot, shoes, walking.

FERRY

If a ferry features in your dream, it hints that your efforts will be rewarded. See also crew, docks, harbor, quay, ship.

FEVER

In dream analysis, fever denotes excitement.

FIELD

The meaning of a dream field depends on its condition. A green field represents prosperity and happiness, while a dry field, or one whose crops are dying or dead, warns of losses. A plowed field tells you that although you have much work ahead, it will be worthwhile. See also corn, farmers, farming, grass, plow.

FIGS

Fresh figs represent sex and the potential for sex to get you into trouble. Dry figs denote financial worries. See also fruit.

FIGHTING

Dreaming of fighting warns that you may soon have to put up a fight. See also attack, battle, blows.

FILES, FILING CABINET

If you see files or a filing cabinet in your dream, you may need to keep better records. See also computer, desk, office.

FILMS

Dreaming of handling films, videos, or similar foretells windfalls, bonuses, and small financial increases. See also camera.

FINGERS

Take note of what happens in your dream if fingers feature in it, because healthy fingers suggest good news, while shriveled fingers or ones that drop off may warn against losses. See also gloves, hand, hands, nails.

Fire engines warn that the fires of passion may lead to regret.

FIRE

Dreaming of a fire generally indicates the fire of passion or fiery emotions. If the fire warms you, all is well, but if it burns you, guard against losing your temper with someone. If you dream of a house on fire, you may soon hear from a friend who needs your help. Setting fire to a house yourself is a sign both of deep anger and the fear that your temper will get the better of you. See also fireplace, flame, furnace, match, smoke.

FIRE ENGINE

If you see a fire engine in your dream, it signals that although you may have a few worries, these should soon clear up. A broken fire engine signifies a loss. If a young woman dreams of riding on a fire engine, she may soon become involved in a sordid affair.

FIREPLACE

In dream symbolism, a fireplace denotes peace and happiness. If a fire is burning brightly in the fireplace, expect an improvement in your love life, but if the fireplace is empty and cold, it augurs the same for amorous relationships. See also fire.

FIREWORKS

Seeing fireworks in your dream hints at the likelihood of a quarrel and being tempted to hit someone.

FISH, FISHING

In dream symbolism, fish usually represent friends, sociability, and lovers. Baiting a hook indicates that you fancy someone and will make an effort to bring yourself to their notice. Dreaming of catching a healthy fish is a good omen because it denotes that you will have influential friends and supporters. Catching a dead fish, however, warns of the loss of wealth and power. Similarly, if you go fishing in your dreams and don't catch anything, this hints that you may lose out on something. Seeing a variety of different fish shows that you will soon be able to take your pick of lovers and friends, while eating fish promises lasting love. See also eels, goldfish, nets, salmon, shark, salmon, trout, whale.

Fish denote love and good friends to come.

F

Dream flames bring success.

FLAME

If the flame burns brightly in your dream, success is indicated. See also candle, fire, match, smoke.

FLASHLIGHT

You may soon see a way through your problems if you dream of a flashlight. See also lamp, lantern.

FLOOD

If a flood features in your dream, it warns that your emotions may become out of control. See also drowning, river, water.

FLOUR

Dreaming of using flour in baking augurs well for a happy domestic life. Buying flour, however, may foretell an illness. See also baker, baking, bread, cakes, dough, doughnut.

FLOWERS

In dream symbolism, flowers signify good news, that is, unless they are crushed, when the outlook is not so good. See also blossoms, chrysanthemums, daffodils, daisy, garden, heather, jasmine, lilac, lily, rose, tulip, violets, wreath.

FLUTE

Hearing a flute's music in a dream denotes happiness in the home, although you may shortly become embarrassed if you dream of playing a flute yourself.

FLYING

Flying dreams are very common, and some interpreters believe that they may be a form of astral projection. There are many ancient interpretations of flying dreams, of which the most positive is that you will rise above your problems and become a high-flyer.

FOG

You may be suffering from obstacles and setbacks in your life if you dream of fog. Seeing fog at sea indicates problems in love, while fog on land denotes a business or financial problem. If the sun burns away the fog, you should overcome your problems.

FOOTBALL

Dreaming of playing football indicates a possible windfall. Watching football warns that you should choose your friends with more care. See also exercise, goal, whistle.

Flowers are messages of good news.

FOREST

If a forest features in your dream, it hints at a happy marriage and well-behaved children, that is, as long as you keep to the straight and narrow. See also trees.

FORK

In dream symbolism, a fork may foretell a separation from a lover. See also knife.

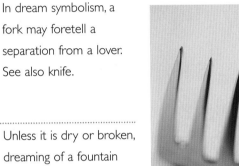

Forks foretell separation.

FOUNTAIN

Unless it is dry or broken, dreaming of a fountain hints at an improvement in your love life. See also water.

FOX

Dreaming of a fox denotes that the success of your plans may be beyond your expectations.

FRIEND

Seeing a friend in your dream usually signals impending good news from friends, but if the friend is in trouble, this may be an omen of precisely that.

FRIES

See chips.

FROG

Dreaming of a frog has a fairy-tale significance: someone unlikely may turn into a handsome prince very soon. See also toad.

FRUIT

If the dream fruit is ripe and succulent, it hints at future prosperity. If it is dried or rotten, however, losses are denoted. See also apple, apricots, cherries, figs, gooseberries, grapes, lemons, nuts, olives, oranges, orchard, pineapple, plums, raspberries, rhubarb, seeds.

FUDGE

Dreaming of making or eating fudge may warn against extravagance. See also chocolate, sweets.

FUNERAL

See burial.

FUR

Wearing fur in a dream denotes future luxury. If the fur is shabby, however, you probably won't enjoy as much luxury as you crave. See also clothing, coat.

FURNACE

If a furnace features in your dream, it hints that people will be grateful for your charitable attitude. See also fire.

FURNITURE

If the furniture in your dream is in good repair, it indicates future happiness, and buying furniture is an even better augury. Dilapidated furniture, however, warns of severe love or marriage problems. See also chair, table.

Dreaming of handsome furniture suggests future happiness.

G

GAG

Dreams in which gags feature are usually obstacle dreams. If you manage to free yourself of the gag, you should soon be able to speak freely and to make progress in your life. If the gag remains in place, however, your present difficulties may continue. Dreaming of gagging someone else indicates that you wish that someone near to you would shut up!

GALLERY

If you dream that you are in an art gallery looking at old masters, an old lover may reappear in your life, while modern paintings denote new friends and lovers. Seeing a sculpture may be telling you to beware of gambling or speculating. If the gallery is a balcony, prosperity is indicated, that is, as long as you don't fall from it. See also art, artists, picture, verandah.

GALLOWS

Seeing a gallows in your dream suggests prosperity and good fortune. See also beheading, execution.

GAMBLING

If you dream that you are gambling, take note of whether you are winning or losing, as this could have implications for how your life will turn out in the near future. See also cards.

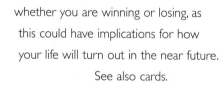

Gambling dreams denote gains or losses.

A garden signifies a haven of peace.

GANGWAY

In dream analysis, a gangway represents your progress in life, so if it leads upward or to somewhere pleasant, you will probably move forward. See also bridge, ship.

GARAGE

If a public garage or parking lot features in your dream, it indicates future prosperity, although a homel garage suggests secrets. See also automobile.

GARDEN

If the dream garden is filled with trees and flowers, this is a good omen, indicating future peace. If the garden is filled with vegetables, however, it augurs less well. See also flowers, hedge, hoe, trees, vegetables, weeds, wheelbarrow.

GARLIC

In dream symbolism, garlic represents prominence and wealth. See also onions.

GAS

Dreaming of gas warns you about an invisible danger, perhaps trouble that could arise if you involve yourself in others' affairs or a brewing scandal. If you dream that you are lighting the gas on a stove, take care not to overextend your finances or credit. If you see someone wearing a gas mask, this indicates that you should attend to matters of finance and credit. Dreaming of an official reading your gas meter suggests that others will interfere in your life or spend your money. Although lighting a gas lamp augurs well for your finances, extinguishing one, or seeing one go out, sends a negative signal regarding your love life. See also gasoline, lamp, lantern.

GASOLINE

In dreams, gasoline signifies danger through fire or an accident. See also gas.

GATE

In dream analysis, a gate may signify the dividing line between this world and the next, and some believe that it indicates the death of someone close to you. If the gate is open, it may also denote opportunities, or, if it is shut, a lack of them. If you unlock the gate or climb over it, it is likely that you will overcome your difficulties. See also door.

GEESE

Seeing geese in your dream is a generally good omen, but if they are cackling, take care that your lover does not talk you into doing something that you are not happy about. See also birds.

GEMS

Dreams that feature any type of gem signify happiness and wealth. See also diamonds, emerald, jewelry, opal, pearls, ruby, sapphire, treasure.

A dream gate may foretell a death around you.

G

GHETTO

Guard against overspending if you dream of being in a ghetto.

GHOST, GHOUL

If the dream ghost is a happy one, your future prospects look bright. A frightening ghost, or one who talks to you, however, may be warning you not to become involved in something that will bring trouble upon your head. There may another reason for dreaming of spirits and ghosts: someone who has "passed over" may trying to contact you.

GIANT

In dream analysis, a giant augurs well for those in business. See also monster, ogre.

GIFT

If you dream that you are given a gift, it may mean that someone who owes you money will pay up or that your love life looks promising. A present may, however, also signify losses that will wipe out previous gains. See also parcel.

GINGER

Dreaming of ginger, be it the color or plant, signifies a passionate, but short-lived, affair.

GIRDLE

In dream symbolism, a girdle represents achievement. See also belt, buckle.

GIRL

Encouraging prospects or surprising news are suggested by the appearance of a girl in your dream. See also child, children, daughter.

GLACIER

Seeing a glacier in your dream may signify the arrival of news from a distance. See also ice, snow.

GLASS

If the dream glass is full, you may soon be hearing from a loved one, but if it is empty, you may face some temporary difficulties. If the glass is broken, it is possible that your wishes will come true. See also cup, mirror, window.

GLOVES

In dream symbolism, gloves indicate that something will need careful handling and that caution is advocated. See also clothes, fingers, hand, hands.

GOAL

Dreaming of scoring a goal suggests that new friends and opportunities will present themselves. See also football.

GOAT

If farmers and gardeners dream of a goat, it may denote that their crops and gardens will flourish. If it features in the dreams of other people, it signifies that they are likely to achieve their ambitions. It may also

Gold foretells financial improvements.

suggest that someone born under the zodiacal sign of Capricorn will become important to you.

GOLD

You may be unusually successful if you handle gold in your dream, and if you are hoping to marry soon, your future spouse may be rich. If your financial position is currently straitened, dreaming of gold suggests that it may soon improve. See also jewelry, money, silver.

GOLDFISH

In dream symbolism, goldfish represent success and a happy relationship. See also fish.

GOLF

Dreaming of golf indicates that although you may have to work alone, you should be successful. See also exercise.

Golf dreams are good news for entrepreneurs.

GONDOLA

A dream gondola hints at romance, perhaps a romantic holiday. See also boat.

GOOSEBERRIES

Whether you dream of raw or cooked gooseberries, they may be warning you not to get yourself into an embarrassing situation. See also fruit.

GOVERNMENT

Be it a local or a national government that appears in your dream, it indicates a period of uncertainty.

GRAIN

See corn.

GRANDPARENTS

In the symbolism of dreams, grandparents signify protection and security. See also old man, old woman, parents.

Grandparents indicate protection and security.

G

GRAPES

Eating grapes in your dream suggests that you have a lot on your mind. Seeing grapes denotes good fortune, and also hints that you will make others happy. See also fruit, vines.

GRASS

If grass features in your dream, it may signify pastures new and fresh experiences. If the grass is healthy, you should prosper and be content. Cutting grass indicates sad news, however. See also field, weeds.

GRASSHOPPER

Dream grasshoppers often represent indecision or conflicting advice.

GRAVE

If you see a grave in your dream, it may be telling you that it is time to put the past behind you and to make a fresh start. Walking on a grave, digging a grave, or seeing the name of someone you know on a gravestone are bad omens that denote sickness and losses, especially in business. See also burial, cemetery.

GREENHOUSE

In dream analysis, a greenhouse hints at love, success, and a bright future.

GUESTS

If you dream of guests, it is possible that your friends will leave you. See also invitation, visiting, visitors.

GUITAR

A dream guitar often signifies that your love life will be happy and your lover faithful.

A guitar signifies a faithful lover.

GUMS

Dreaming of having sore gums indicates family and personal problems. See also teeth.

GUN

Seeing a gun in your dream denotes either real physical danger or the danger of your life running into trouble: the loss of your job or a quarrel, for example. You would be well advised to look around you and to take care. See also ammunition.

Weapon dreams warn of danger.

GYPSY

If a gypsy features in your dream, you should take note of any offers that come your way. He or she may also foretell moving house or traveling. See also clairvoyant.

H

HAIR

In dreams, hair that is in good condition is a sign of prosperity, joy, good health, and happiness. Neatly cut and groomed hair hints at an improvement in your status and finances, as well as good friends. If the hair is thin, weak, or falling out, it warns that hard times may be on the way, while hair that turns gray and falls out foretells illness. Dreams of combing hair foretell a proposal of marriage, but also possible sickness, while flower-bedecked hair suggests that your problems won't be as bad as you think.

The color of the hair is significant. Blond hair indicates love, brown or black hair signifies success in business, while red hair suggests that someone will denounce you. Gray hair is said to be an omen of death, while comparing one white and one black hair indicates that you will soon have to make a choice. See also barber, beard.

A dream handshake brings help from influential people.

HALL

If you dream of a narrow hall, you may have financial difficulties. If the hallway is large and impressive, your plans should succeed.

HAND, HANDS

The meaning of a dream in which a hand features depends on the condition of the hand. If it is beautiful, it may signify either that you will prosper or that help is at hand. Hands that are tied suggest that you won't be able to make any changes just yet, although handcuffs hint at good fortune. Blood on the hands warns that your family will reject you, while hairy hands suggest that you will not rise to an elevated position, and even that you may spend time in prison. Seeing a right hand signifies that the dream may be sending you a message about your father, or alternatively, if you dream about a left hand, your mother. Shaking hands indicates help from influential people. See also fingers, gloves, nails.

H

Handwriting tells you to keep your lover on dry land!

HANDKERCHIEF

Most handkerchief dreams augur badly in some way. A dirty or bloodstained handkerchief indicates a quarrel, while a linen one warns of hidden hostility, and losses in either business or love are signified by a lost handkerchief. Only a silk handkerchief has positive significance, hinting as it does at a happy surprise. See also nose.

HANDWRITING

One old source of dream meanings states that if you dream of handwriting, your lover will shortly fall out of a boat, so perhaps it would be best not to take any romantic cruises for a while! See also ink, paper, pencil, writing.

HARBOR

In dreams, harbors symbolize good news, as well as the seeking and finding of a safe place. See also docks, quay, ship.

HARE

Dreaming of killing a hare denotes temporary upsets, while cooking and eating it foretell a happy family life. Seeing a hare running away indicates a move of house. See also animals, rabbit.

HARMONICA

Dream harmonicas represent fun and parties.

HARP

In the symbolism of dreams, a harp denotes an ending or a parting, especially if a string breaks. If you dream of playing a harp, your lover may soon leave you.

HARPOON

Dreaming of a harpoon hints at an increase in your income.

HARVEST

Dreaming of a good harvest is one of the most auspicious dreams that you could have. Only if the harvest is poor is there an indication of financial or emotional insecurity to come. See also corn, fall, farmer, field.

In dreams, harvest foretells prosperity.

HAT

Unless it is lost, a dream hat is a good omen for business people. See also cap, clothes.

HATCHET

In dream analysis, a hatchet signifies danger or losses. See also pickax.

HAWK

Dreaming of a flying hawk indicates a bright future, but if the hawk is roosting, life may be boring for a while. See also birds.

HEAD

In general, dreaming of a head advises you either to keep your head or not to allow anything to go to your head. Dreaming of a swollen head tells you to beware of becoming overconfident, while dreaming of having an animal's head may be warning you not to become involved in a destructive sexual liaison. If your head is turned back to front in your dream, it may be signaling that you'd better get out of the country fast! See also beheading.

HEART

If you dream of having a pain in your heart, you may actually be suffering the early stages of a heart attack, so monitor the situation carefully and if necessary consult your doctor. Less worryingly, it may signify that love surrounds you, although you would still be advised to watch your health. See also love.

HEATHER

Dream heather signifies good luck, especially if it is white. See also flowers.

HEAVEN

Dreaming of heaven augurs well for this life, as well as the next. See also angel, hell.

HEDGE

If you dream that you are cutting a hedge, it hints at good fortune, but if you are jumping over one, you may end up with something that you didn't want. See also garden.

HEDGEHOG

In the symbolism of dreams, a hedgehog warns that your kindness will be taken advantage of.

HELL

Dreaming of hell advises you to take care in every respect. See also devil, heaven.

HENS

Dream hens represent family reunions. See also chickens, cocks.

A dream heart sends a health warning.

H

HERMIT

If a hermit features in your dream, you may be well advised to retreat, reflect, and develop some spiritual insight in order to find the help and advice that you seek.

HILL

Seeing a hill in your dream suggests that you are making progress, although the steeper and stonier the hill, the harder your ascent will be. See also mountain.

HIVE

In dreams, hives symbolize prosperity and lack of worries. See also bees, honey.

HOE

Wielding a hoe in your dream foretells good health and high spirits, but also denotes that there is much work to be done. See also garden.

HOLLY

Dreaming of holly generally hints at good fortune in terms of money and friends. If the holly pricks you, however, it may be administering a warning that you should avoid becoming involved in others' schemes and intrigues. See also ivy, mistletoe.

HOME

If your home features in your dream, it usually signifies that you are yearning for protection and comfort. Even if it is not the one that you are currently living in, dreaming of your home indicates your state of mind at the time of the dream, as well as your hopes and fears for the future. If your dream home is attractive and peaceful, it is likely that your life is also tranquil, but if it is chaotic, you may need to rethink your present and future circumstances. See also house, mortgage, neighbors, removal.

HONEY

In the symbolism of dreams, honey indicates both wealth and a sweet life. See also bees, hive.

HORN

Dream horns of any kind denote delusions of grandeur.

HOROSCOPE

See zodiac.

HORSE

Generally speaking, dreams in which a horse features are auspicious if the horse is fit and healthy, but inauspicious if it is thin and worn out. If you see a black horse that is strong, business should be good, but if it is ailing, disappointment is indicated, while if the dream horse is brown, it foretells stagnation and delays. If the horse is gray, you may face a time of restlessness and uncertainty, but if it is white, it promises financial progress. A stallion signifies prosperity and a better situation in life. Dreaming of a horse being shod hints at excellent marriage prospects and unexpected financial windfalls.

If you dream that you are riding a well-behaved horse, good fortune is indicated, but if it is bucking or kicking you, it is possible that your lover will let you down. Riding slowly warns that whatever it is that you are doing won't come to fruition, while riding quickly suggests that you will obtain your heart's desire, but that you will have to endure some bumpy times before you do so. Galloping usually signifies success. See also hunt, jockey, saddle, stable, wagon, whip.

HORSESHOE

Unless the horseshoe in your dream is broken, it foretells good luck and an enjoyable journey.

HOSPITAL

Dreaming of a hospital advises you that you may either be in need of treatment of some sort or of hospitality. See also doctor, illness, medicine, nurse, operation, surgeon, X-ray.

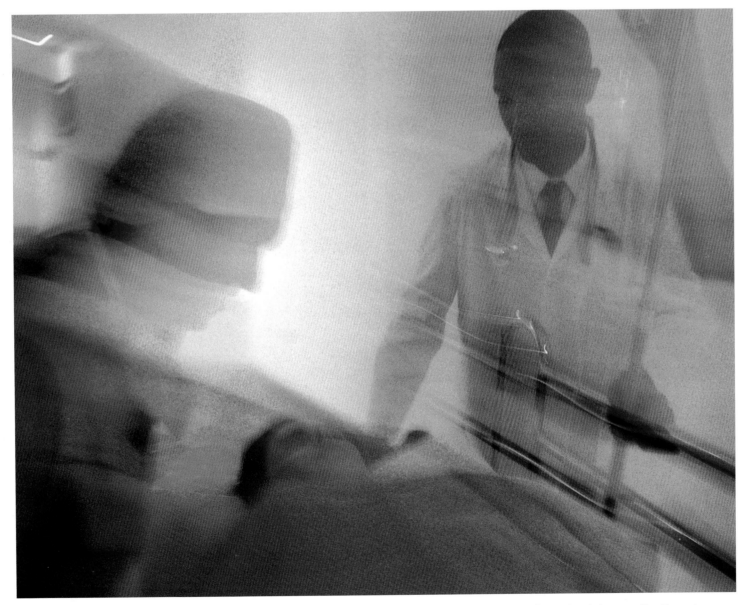

Dream hospitals warn of health worries.

HOTEL

If you dream of being alone in a hotel, the dream usually relates to your social status and business affairs, while dreaming of being in a hotel with another person relates to your love life. A luxurious hotel augurs well, but if it is a dump, expect problems. If the hotel is crowded, your dream may be telling you to try to stand apart from the crowd.

HOURGLASS

In the symbolism of dreams, an hourglass signifies that time is running out for you in some area of your life. See also watch.

HOUSE

Changes in your circumstances are foretold if you dream of a house, and the type and condition of the house will tell you whether you will be heading upward or downward. The dream house may also reflect your state of mind, so if it is peaceful, you are too, but if it is noisy, dirty or chaotic, you may need to take stock of your situation and lifestyle. See also home, mansion, mortgage, neighbors, removal, rent, roof, verandah.

Hurricane dreams denote quarrels.

HUNTING

Hunt dreams are typically obstacle dreams, and the way in which the hunt unfolds usually reflects your current state of mind. See also horse.

HURRICANE

In dream analysis, a hurricane denotes quarrels and strife. See also storm, wind.

HUSBAND

A husband is a positive thing to dream of, particularly if you are hoping to find one! If you already have a husband, good news for the family is hinted at. If the dream husband is ill or unhappy, however, trouble may be brewing. See also man, marriage, wedding.

This dream tells you to wait until the ice melts.

I

ICE

Dreaming of ice signifies that some aspect your life has been frozen for the time being. See also glacier, skating, snow.

ICE CREAM

Happiness for the family, as well as prosperity, is foretold if you dream of ice cream. See also Jell-O.

IDIOT

If an idiot features in your dream, it is usually a contrary dream that indicates that either you or other people are brighter than you think.

ILLNESS

Dreaming of illness often warns of actual sickness or else of future troubles. See also asthma, bronchitis, doctor, hospital, medicine, nurse, pain, plague, ulcer, vomit.

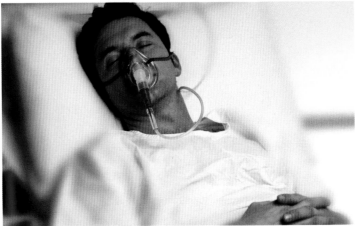

Illness dreams indicate health worries.

INCOME

Dreaming of an increase in your income is usually a contrary dream that denotes exactly the opposite, and vice versa. See also money.

INCOME TAX

You are probably worrying about loans and money matters if income tax features in your dream..

INK

Dreaming of spilling ink augurs well for your future prosperity, while making a inkblot or using a blotter sends a warning about a possible betrayal. Pouring ink into an inkstand may foretell a period of travel. See also handwriting, paper, writing.

INSANITY

Dreaming of insanity of any kind often hints that your plans may succeed, however crazy they may seem.

INSURANCE

If you dream of buying insurance, it is probable that you are being reminded to do so when you awake. Dreaming of cashing in on an insurance policy augurs badly for your finances, however. See also money.

INVITATION

Receiving a dream invitation hints that a party is in the air, which may not live up to your expectations.

ISLAND

Enjoyable journeys and a happy marriage are signified by any type of dream island.

IVY

Dreaming of ivy suggests that your business, as well as your health, will improve, although you may have to put your love life on the back burner while you concentrate on your work. See also holly, mistletoe.

J

JACKDAW

Seeing a jackdaw in your dream may warn of ill health, quarrels, or a death. See also birds.

JAM

See preserves.

JASMINE

In dream symbolism, jasmine signifies good luck or a happy marriage. See also flowers.

JAWS

If jaws feature in your dream, you may become the victim of gossip. See also teeth.

JEALOUSY

Interpreting jealousy dreams is straightforward: either you will become jealous of someone or someone will become jealous of you.

JELL-O, JELLY

In dreams, Jjell-O generally hints at pleasant reunions. One old interpretation asserts that dreaming of Jell-O means that your child will have weak ankles! See also ice cream.

JESTER

A dream jester may be telling you not to be silly.

JET

Dreaming of jet jewelry indicates sad news, while dreaming of a jet plane suggests that you need to get away for a while and perhaps take a holiday. See also airplane, jewelry.

JEWELRY

Unless it is broken, jewelry in dreams often signals an increase in income. See also earrings, engagement ring, gems, gold, jet, necklace, pearls, ring, silver.

The dream juggler offers opportunities.

J

JOB

If you are looking for a job in your dream, but can't find one, it is possible that your circumstances will improve. If you do find a job, however, be careful that you don't end up losing your current one.

JOCKEY

A dream jockey represents an unexpected gift. See also horse.

JOURNEY

In the symbolism of dreams, a journey denotes a change of circumstances, possibly through travel. Note whether the journey is smooth or bumpy, as this will indicate what you are facing.

JUGGLER

If your dream features a juggler, it advises you to accept opportunities when they are offered. See also conjurer.

JUNGLE

A dream jungle warns you not to become involved in something that will ultimately harm you, and is a particularly poor omen for financial matters.

JURY

You may be in need of a change of job if you dream of a jury. See also attorney, advocate, justice, lawyer, lawsuit.

JUSTICE

In dream analysis, justice in any guise denotes undue criticism. Dreaming of the scales of justice augurs well for a successful future. See also attorney, advocate, jury, lawyer, police.

Dreaming of justice warns that either this or injustice may be on the way.

K

KANGAROO

Dreaming of a kangaroo hints that you will outwit your enemies.

KENNEL

If a kennel features in your dream, it indicates that someone whom you would like to have as a friend isn't responding to your charm. See also bulldog, dog.

KETTLE

In the symbolism of dreams, a kettle signifies domestic happiness and an attractive home. See also boil, boiling, tea, teapot, teacups.

KEY

Tradition suggests that if you dream of a key, you may fail in an important interview, but a key may also indicate a new home or the key to an idea. The interpretation may vary according to the scenario that is envisaged in the dream. Finding a key, for example, denotes finding a solution to a problem, while losing one indicates disappointment and a loss of friendship. Being given a key signifies that your home life may improve, and keeping a key suggests a future position of responsibility. A key may also symbolize love,

A dream key has many interpretations.

especially when it is inserted into a lock. If a key is given away, it warns that you may lose your good name, and a broken key suggests that you are about to throw away a chance of success. See also door, doorbell, keyhole.

KEYHOLE

You would be well advised to keep an eye on what others are doing if your dream features a keyhole. In addition, you may be facing an obstacle. See also key.

KILL

Dreaming of killing someone hints at a successful financial "killing." See also death.

KING

In the symbolism of dreams, a king signifies that your ambition may pay off and that you may receive great honors. See also cards, coronation, crown, emperor, palace, queen, prince, princess.

K

KISS

Dream kisses generally symbolize joyful reunions, love, happiness, and a satisfying family life. Kissing the wrong person in your dream, however, could be warning you not to fall in love with the wrong person. Rather surprisingly, dreaming of a woman kissing another woman is regarded by many analysts as representing fertility! See also love.

KITCHEN

Unless it is bare, or in a mess, dreaming of a kitchen usually augurs well for the future. See also cooking, oven, room, saucepan.

KITTEN

Dream kittens are generally telling you that it is time to let your hair down and have some fun. See also cat.

Knife dreams warn of danger.

KNIFE

Dream knives are usually bad omens that may warn of real danger or of being metaphorically stabbed in the back. They may foretell any number of unpleasant things, including separation, surgery, and enemies. See also dagger, fork, operation, surgeon, sword.

KNITTING

Dreaming that you are knitting denotes success, but if someone else is doing the knitting, deception may be indicated. See also embroidery, needle, sewing, yarn.

KNOT

In the symbolism of dreams, a knot indicates that you can't get something to work as you would like it to. If you become so frustrated that you cut the knot in your dream, it denotes the end of a friendship or amorous relationship.

A keyhole suggests that you need to keep an eye on things.

L

LABORATORY

A dream laboratory may warn of danger or sickness. See also microscope.

LABYRINTH

Dreaming of a labyrinth or maze is common, and suggests that your life is filled with difficulties. The message may be to look at your situation and, if you can, to go back and start again. If you find your way out of the labyrinth, this hints that you will solve your problems, but if you don't, they will probably continue for a while longer.

LACE

In the symbolism of dreams, lace denotes popularity with the opposite sex. See also clothes, silk, velvet.

LADDER

A dream ladder represents your path through life, both at present and in the future. You may succeed in your plans if you climb the ladder successfully, but you probably won't reach your goal if you can't climb very far. Getting to the top of the ladder is the best augury, but even climbing down one is auspicious if it gets you out of trouble. Dreaming of a ladder falling on you warns of shocks and disappointments, while carrying a ladder for someone else suggests that you will help them to get on in life. Feeling dizzy on a ladder denotes that you are taking on more than you can cope with. See also escalator, stairs.

LAKE

If the lake in your dream is smooth and placid, it suggests that life will be good for you in the future. If it is rough and turbulent, however, things may not be easy for a while. Dreaming of sailing on a smooth, clear lake denotes making good friends and enjoying a happy life, but a muddy or rocky lake bed indicate difficulties. See also boat, pond, water.

The meaning of a lamb dream depends on the condition of the lamb.

LAMB

If the lamb that features in your dream appears content, it indicates that you will probably be happy, but if it is in distress, you may end up feeling like a lamb going to slaughter. If it has a bloodstained fleece, the lamb foretells that innocent people may suffer as a result of someone else's wrongdoing. See also sheep, shepherds.

LAMP, LANTERN

In the symbolism of dreams, a lamp or lantern denotes enlightenment. See also flashlight, gas.

LAUGHING

Unless the laughter in your dream is mocking, when it may signify illness and disappointment, laughter symbolizes success, happiness, and good health.

LION

If a lion features in your dream, it suggests that although you may take the lead in an important enterprise, you should beware of lurking enemies. See also animals.

LIQUOR

In dreams, liquor sometimes tells you to beware of taking something that is not yours and also to prevent anyone else from doing so. If the liquor is stored in barrels, it signifies prosperity. See also bar.

LOBSTER

You may soon be in a position of command if you dream of a lobster. See also crab.

LOCK

See keyhole.

LOG

Dreaming of sawing logs denotes an improvement in your domestic situation. Indeed, any type of dream log augurs well for your love and family life. See also carpenter, saw, trees.

LOVE

Dreams of love suggest that you will be loved, however the love manifests itself, be it as family love, romantic love, the love of a friend, or any other kind of love. See also heart, kiss, valentine.

LUGGAGE

When I was married to my difficult first husband, I frequently dreamed about luggage, but I have never had luggage dreams since I got together with my second husband. It will therefore probably not come as a surprise to you to learn that dreaming of luggage denotes unhappiness, especially within marriage.

If you are carrying your own luggage, you may have become so unhappy that you are beyond even speaking to anyone else about it. Although losing your luggage may denote an inheritance, it may also have some bearing on your frame of mind, in that you may feel that your life is spiraling out of control and that you have lost the ability to provide for yourself and your family. In some cases, dreaming of luggage may indicate a long journey to come.

Love means . . . love!

Dreams of luggage signify unhappiness.

LAWYER, LAWSUIT

When a lawyer or lawsuit features in your dream, you may be advised to solicit some specialist advice, which may be legal. See also attorney, jury, justice.

LEMONS

Some dream interpreters suggest that lemons symbolize arguments. See also fruit, oranges.

LEOPARD

Dreaming of a leopard may be warning you to beware of enemies.

LETTER

Dream letters have many different interpretations. A letter may sometimes suggest that money matters and long-distance business may soon become important, although it may also denote jealousy in love or the imminent arrival of bad news. See also envelope, mailman.

Letters bring news in dreams, as in life.

Lightning dreams suggest a move of house.

LIGHTHOUSE

In dream symbolism, a lighthouse signifies riding out a storm. See also storm, water.

LIGHTNING

If you dream of lightning, it could presage a house move. See also oak, storm, thunder, thunderbolt.

LILAC

You may soon lose a friend if you dream of lilac, although this will probably turn out to be a blessing in disguise. See also flowers.

LILY

Some traditions regard dreaming of a lily as a warning of future illness, but others see it as symbolizing contentment in love and an elevated social status. See also flowers.

MAGGOTS

Seeing maggots in a dream warns that troubles may crawl out to confront you. See also worms.

MAGIC

Dreams that feature magic of any kind denote pleasant surprises and enjoyable travels. See also conjurer, witch, wizard.

MAGNET

In the symbolism of dreams, a magnet signifies either being drawn to a member of the opposite sex or having the ability to attract one.

MAGPIE

An old song about seeing, or dreaming about, magpies runs, "One for sorrow, two for joy, three for a girl, and four for a boy." Other interpretations suggest that if you are not getting anywhere with someone you fancy, it is time to give up trying. See also birds, crows, ravens.

MAILMAN

A dream mailman signifies that news is on its way, and how you felt in the dream should indicate whether it will be the kind of news that you want to receive or not. See also envelope, letter.

MAN

The meaning of a dream that features a man depends on the type of man and what he is doing. If a woman dreams about a man who is kind and attractive, he may denote

Maps show that you need change.

good fortune and a prospective lover, but if he is ugly or bad tempered, his appearance is not a good omen. See also husband.

MANSION

Promotion and wealth are signified if you dream about a mansion. It may also denote that your home will suit you. See also house, palace.

MAP

If you dream of a map, it may indicate a coming journey, but may also be telling you that you are feeling restless and need a change. See also atlas.

MARCHING

You may be yearning to join a large firm or organization, such as the armed forces, if marching features in your dream. See also army, soldier.

MARKET

If you work in sales, or have something to sell, a dream market is a good omen. See also store.

M

MARRIAGE

When trying to interpret a dream that involved marriage, consider the content of the dream. If the marriage was to a good-looking and well-mannered partner, it is likely that your partnership will be fine, but if it was to an ugly or rude partner, it may not be a success. If you dreamed that you attended a wedding, successful business affairs are denoted. In some circumstances, dreaming of marriage may foretell news of a death. See also bride, bridegroom, bridesmaid, husband, wedding.

MARSH

In dream analysis, a marsh represents an unseen danger.

MASK

If you see a mask in your dream, it may be warning you that a friend cannot be relied upon. If you are wearing the mask, it may suggest that you are having difficulties making others understand you.

MAST

A dream mast is usually trying to point out something that you can't, or won't, see. It may also be a travel indicator, however; if so, and it is in good repair, the journey should be pleasant, but if the mast is damaged, it may not be so smooth. See also ship.

MAT

Be careful where you tread, and think carefully about what you are doing, if you see a mat in your dream. See also carpets, door, doorbell.

MATCH

In the language of dreams, seeing someone striking a match hints at good news. See also fire, flame, smoke, tobacco.

MASS

Dreaming of attending a mass augurs well for the future. See also church.

MAZE

See labyrinth.

MEAT

If the meat that appears in your dream is raw, it indicates that you will get what you want. If it is cooked, however, your heart's desire will fall to someone else instead. Roast meat often symbolizes affection and friendship. See also beef, butcher.

MECHANIC

A dream mechanic hints at success at work or a house move. See also automobile, garage.

Who is hiding behind the mask?

Medicine dreams indicate that something is not right.

MEDICINE

You may soon be putting something right if you dream of medicine of any kind. See also doctor, drugs, hospital, illness, nurse, syringe.

MERMAID

A dream mermaid suggests that you may be hankering after a former lover.

MERRY-GO-ROUND

If you are riding on a merry-go-round with others, especially children, in your dream, a period of happiness is foretold. If you are alone, however, the merry-go-round denotes that although you will be feeling fed up and downhearted for a while, sooner or later your circumstances will change for the better.

METEOR

Loss, as well as problems that come out of the blue, are indicated if a meteor streaks across your dream. See also comet, shooting star, sky, star.

MICROSCOPE

In the symbolism of dreams, a microscope represents the discovery of talents and the learning of new skills. If the microscope is broken, challenges and problems are indicated. See also laboratory.

MILESTONE

Dreaming of a milestone often tells you that you are approaching an important point in your life. See also road, signpost.

MILK

Dreaming of milk is said by many interpreters to presage extraordinarily good luck, happiness, and prosperity, such as an outstanding harvest for farmers. If the milk has been spilled or spoiled, it still retains its positive significance, although to a lesser degree. See also cattle.

MILL

In dream analysis, a mill represents peace and prosperity. See also corn.

MILLIONAIRE

If a woman dreams of a millionaire, it may presage marriage to a man who was once rich, but is no longer. See also abundance, affluence, money, riches.

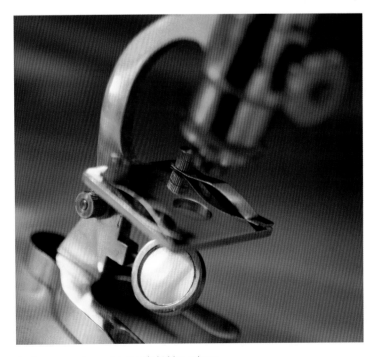

In dreams, a microscope reveals hidden talents.

M

MINE

Dreaming of a mine hints at great untapped wealth. See also coal mine, pit, quarry.

MINT

An improvement in someone's health may be denoted if a mint features in a dream. See also candy.

MIRROR

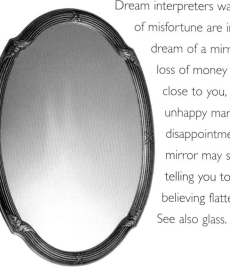

Dream interpreters warn that all kinds of misfortune are indicated if you dream of a mirror, perhaps the loss of money or of someone close to you, bad friends, an unhappy marriage, or disappointments in general. A mirror may sometimes also be telling you to beware of believing flattery or being vain. See also glass.

MISTLETOE

Good relationships in the future are promised if you dream of mistletoe. See also holly, ivy, Christmas.

MOLE

If the dream mole is an animal, it may be telling you that someone is undermining your position. Moles on the face and body have great significance, and you are advised to consult a specialist book on face-reading or moles to discover them all. Moles on the right side of the forehead, for example, represent problems regarding your relationship with your father, while on the left side they indicate problems with your mother. A mole on your back signifies that although you may have to work hard throughout your life, success may be your reward.

Money dreams denote financial ups or downs.

MONEY

If you find money in your dream, difficulties may be on the horizon, while if you lose money, your plans may succeed beyond your wildest expectations. Counting money signifies that gains are on the way, and spending money denotes losses. If you dream that you find, or are given, gold, or that you are giving money away, your future may well be prosperous. See also counting, dollar, gold, income, income tax, insurance, millionaire, mortgage, poverty, purse, silver, riches, treasure, wages, wallet.

MONK

A dream monk foretells trouble in the family. See also abbey.

Dream monks bring family troubles.

MONKEY

A marriage or new partnership is hinted at if a monkey appears in your dream.

MONSTER

If the monster chases you in your dream, it indicates that you have something to worry about, but if you kill it, or see it off, you may be successful. See also dragon, giant, ogre, vampire.

MOON

Seeing the moon in a dream, or seeing things by moonlight, is usually interpreted as indicating that you are not seeing a situation clearly. The rest of the dream may well advise you on the best course of action. See also eclipse, night, observatory, sky, star, sun, zodiac.

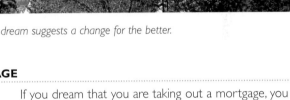

A mountain dream suggests a change for the better.

MORTGAGE

If you dream that you are taking out a mortgage, you probably need to budget more carefully. See also home, house, money.

MOTHER, MOTHER-IN-LAW

Dreaming of a mother or mother-in-law is generally a positive sign, especially for business, travel, and relationships with friends. See also father, father-in-law, parents.

MOUNTAIN

In the language of dreams, a mountain represents a change in your life that, with a bit of effort, will turn out successfully. See also hill.

MOUSE

A dream mouse promises good news and celebrations. If you kill a mouse in your dream, you may overcome an enemy. See also rat, vermin.

MUSHROOMS

Dreaming of mushrooms hints that small surprises are on the way. See also vegetables.

In dreams, the moon suggests a lack of clarity.

N

Dream nails signify achievements.

NAILS

Dreaming of fingernails indicates that you will achieve your goals if you work hard and have a little help from others. See also fingers.

NAKEDNESS

Traditional interpretations suggest that dreaming of nakedness denotes financial losses, but this kind of dream also implies fear and vulnerability, and may be warning you that your life is becoming out of control in some way. If you have a habit of hiding your true self from others, this dream may also reveal your fear of being caught out. See also clothes, undressing.

NAVY

Dreaming of being in a naval ship suggests that you will have a fight on your hands. If the ship is in good condition, you should win the battle, but if it is dilapidated, you may find it difficult to prevail. See also admiral, ship.

NECKLACE

Although dreaming of being given a necklace may presage a happy marriage, wearing one may denote an unhappy marriage to a wealthy partner. (Misery in comfort, perhaps?) If you dream of breaking a necklace, the bonds of either a loveless marriage or one that brought extreme poverty, may soon be broken. See also jewelry.

NEEDLE

If you dream of a needle, it often reveals that you are a hard-working, sensible person, as well as someone who has good friends. See also embroidery, knitting, pins, sewing, tailor, thimble.

NEIGHBORS

In the symbolism of dreams, neighbors represent gossip. Whether you are the one who is enjoying a good old gossiping session with your neighbors in your dream, or whether it is they who are gossiping behind your back, should be revealed by the course of the dream. See also home, house.

NEST

A dream nest typically refers to your home, and often indicates a house move. If the nest is empty, you may be alone in your new home and may feel as though your life is equally empty, but if it is full of eggs or birds, there are plenty of people around you and your life will seem pleasant and fulfilling. See also birds, eggs.

NETS

Dreaming of fishing nets may simply denote that there will be a change in the weather! It can also be a warning, however, that you should be honest in your dealings with others. See also fish, fishing.

NETTLES

If the nettles in your dream don't sting you, they hint that you will be prosperous, but if they do, not only may you be unhappy, but you will make others miserable, too.

NEWSPAPER

News is likely to be on its way if you dream of a newspaper, but whether it is good or bad news depends on how you felt while you were dreaming. See also obituary.

NIGHT

Dreaming of night may denote that you are being kept in the dark. See also moon, sky, stars.

NIGHTMARE

Nightmares, which come in many forms, may be warnings, outlets for feelings of stress, indications of fear, or comments on your lifestyle.

NOSE

Dreaming that your nose is growing may be indicating that your power and status are increasing, and vice versa if it is shrinking. Hair growing on your nose suggests that your life may soon take an unusual turn, while a bleeding nose foretells a shock or disaster. See also faces, handkerchief.

NUDITY

See nakedness.

NURSE

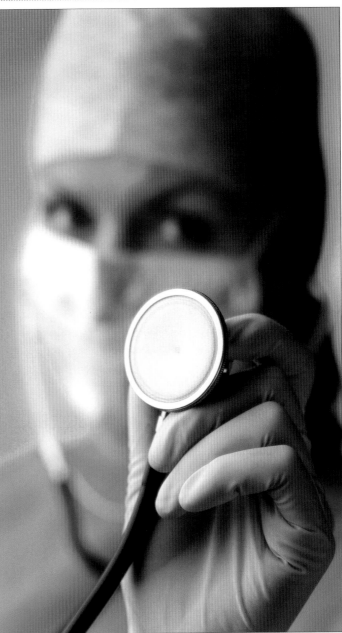

If the dream nurse approaches you, illness may on the way, but if he or she is leaving you, it augurs well for your health, as well as the health of your loved ones. See also doctor, hospital, illness, medicine, operation.

NUTS

Dreams about nuts relate to future prosperity. See also fruit.

O

OAK

If the oak is in good condition in your dream, riches and honors are denoted, and if it is heavy with acorns, a promotion and pay rise may be on the way. An oak tree also augurs well for those in love. However, if the oak is split and dying, or if it has been struck by lightning, you may be in for a nasty surprise. See also acorns, trees.

OAR

Dreaming of handling oars suggests that you will have to set aside your own wishes in order to help others. If you have lost an oar, it denotes that someone may soon leave your family circle. See also boat.

OATS

In the language of dreams, oats represent prosperity. Wild oats? Well, you don't need me to interpret this for you, do you? See also corn.

OBITUARY

A dream in which an obituary features may be a contrary dream, so if you are reading a friend's obituary in your dream, they may be getting married before too long. See also dead people, death, newspaper, will.

OBSERVATORY

Dreaming of an observatory may indicate that you need to look up from your present circumstances or that you may wish to study or gain new skills. See also moon, sky, star.

OCEAN

In dream analysis, an ocean relates to your emotions. If the ocean is serene, you will probably be calm and happy, but if it is stormy, your emotions may soon be in turmoil. See also sailing, water.

OFFICE

Dreaming of being in an office is probably simply a way of sorting out work problems in your sleep. Dreaming of being out of the office, however, suggests that something may soon be stolen or taken away from you. See also computer, desk, files, filing cabinet.

OGRE

Fear of your father or an authority figure may be indicated if you dream of an ogre. See also giant, monster.

OLD MAN, OLD WOMAN

Seeing an old man or woman in your dream is a sign of increasing wisdom. See also grandparents.

Better to dream of a healthy oak than an ailing one.

A stormy ocean indicates stormy relationships.

OLIVES

In the language of dreams, anything to do with olives or olive trees symbolizes contentment and merry times with friends and relatives. The only downside is if you break a jar of olives, as this denotes a disappointment just when you think that everything is going well. See also fruit, trees.

ONIONS

Dream onions are related to spite and envy. Either you are being the spiteful one or someone else may be being nasty to you. See also garlic, vegetables.

OPAL

Good luck and a happy marriage are denoted when an opal features in your dream. See also gems.

OPERA

If you see an opera in your dream, it may be a warning that your lover is both boastful and a shameless flatterer. See also concert, orchestra, play.

OPERATION

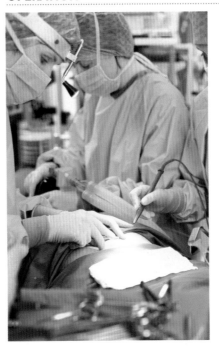

If you are undergoing the dream operation, you may soon be successful, but if anyone else is being operated on, unexpected news may be coming your way. See also doctor, hospital, knife, nurse, surgeon.

OPIUM

Dreaming of opium warns that others may take advantage of you. See also drugs.

O

ORANGES

Seeing orange trees in a dream signals good health and a comfortable home. Eating oranges denotes that a friend may become ill, or that colleagues at work may become dissatisfied. See also fruit, lemons.

ORCHARD

In dream symbolism, an orchard represents success, peace, and prosperity. See also fruit, trees.

ORCHESTRA

A dream orchestra may be advising you to keep in tune with those around you. See also concert, opera.

ORGAN

Hearing a church organ in a dream is an auspicious sign for love and happiness. See also cathedral, church.

ORPHAN

Strangers may help you if you dream of an orphan. See also child, children.

OSTRICH

Dreaming of an ostrich suggests that although you will attract wealth, your relationships will suffer, while if you catch an ostrich, travel is signified. See also birds.

OVEN

Unless the oven in your dream is broken, in which case your children may be aggravating, you should be loved by your family. See also baker, baking, cooking, kitchen.

OWL

In the language of dreams, an owl symbolizes wisdom. See also birds.

OXEN

If you dream of seeing a well-fed ox, it hints that your status within your community will rise. Oxen grazing in green fields suggest future wealth and/or marriage to a rich partner, while if they are drinking from a clear pool, true love may soon come your way. A dead ox, however, warns of bereavement. See also plow, yoke.

OYSTERS

If you are in business, dreaming of oysters foretells a lot of future work. In addition, because oysters are said to be aphrodisiacs, dreaming of them may well be telling you something about the state of your sex life. See also pearls.

The owl represents wisdom.

A dream palace denotes a good marriage.

PAIN

Dreams of pain refer to family members who may upset you, but sometimes also to exile. See also agony, illness.

PALACE

If a palace features in your dream, it hints at an improvement in your prospects and circumstances through marriage. It does not augur so well for health, however. See also king, mansion, prince, princess, queen.

PALM TREE

If a young woman dreams of a palm tree, it may denote a cheerful and pleasant future husband. If the palm tree is dying, however, then love may be, too. See also trees.

PANCAKE

Dreaming of eating pancakes indicates unexpected success. See also eggs.

PAPER

If the paper in your dream is clean, it suggests that your status may rise, but if it is dirty or written on, you may suffer an injustice. See also ink, pencil, writing.

PARACHUTE

A dream parachute offers a way out of a tricky situation. See also airplane, sky.

PARCEL

In the language of dreams, a parcel represents an unexpected event that is more likely to be bad than good. See also gift.

PARENTS

If your parents appear happy in your dream, then good luck may be coming their way, while your own work should go well. If they appear unhappy or sick, however, it augurs badly for both them and you. See also father, father-in-law, grandparents, mother, mother-in-law.

PARROT

A dream parrot is warning you to beware of giving away secrets. See also birds.

PARTING

In dreams, a parting symbolises a few small problems. See also crossroads.

PARTY

If your dream is a party, take it that some fun is likely to be on the way.

P

The dream path is the path of life.

PATH

Dreams of paths, roadways, alleys, and even staircases, all have the same root, in that they refer to your path in life. If the path is clear, wide, and sunny, and you have no difficulty in going along it, all should be well. When the path is rough, muddy, stony, or difficult to walk along, however, it indicates that your life will not be easy for a while. See also alley, escalator, ladder, road, stairs.

PEACOCK

Some dream analysts suggest that dream peacocks indicate wealth for the family. See also birds.

PEARLS

If you dream of single pearls or an intact string of pearls, they denote a great social life, money, and a lot of fun to come. If a pearl necklace breaks, however, jealousy may mar your relationship. See also gems, jewelry, oysters.

PEAS

Dream peas hint that small amounts of money will come your way. See also vegetables.

PENCIL

If a pencil features in your dream, it suggests that you will have a good job that you will enjoy. See also handwriting, paper, writing.

PENGUIN

In the language of dreams, a penguin indicates that although you have ambitions, someone or something is holding you back. See also birds.

PEPPER

Dreaming about pepper in any shape or form, including red, orange, or green peppers (capsicums), warns that you may become the subject of gossip. Grinding pepper suggests that you will become the victim of a malicious person, while a pepper pot foretells quarrels. If you dream that a young woman is seasoning her food with pepper, her friends may deceive her. See also salt, vegetables.

P

A pencil denotes a good job.

PIANO

If a piano appears in your dream, you may soon either find something that you have lost or have it returned to you.

PICKAX

If you dream of a pickax, look out, as there may be enemies about! See also hatchet.

PICKLES

Dreaming of eating pickles generally denotes problems in love and rivals for your lover's affections.

I feel that I should make a personal observation here, because I have known women who have dreamt about pickles when in the early stages of pregnancy or shortly before going into labor. In early pregnancy, this is probably because the body craves acid when it is building up amino acids for the baby to float around

in. The dreams of, or cravings for, pickles before labor seem to be caused by the body's requirement for certain acids that have the ability to kick-start the hormonal changes that are needed to induce the process of labor.

PICNIC

A dream picnic hints that you will become the center of attention. If you meet a nice person of the opposite sex at the picnic, it may presage a wonderful love affair or marriage.

PICTURE

Whether the picture in your dream is a painting or a photograph, it augurs badly, and the more you admire the picture, the worse the prospects seem. You would be advised to prepare yourself for treachery and betrayal. See also album, art, artists, gallery.

PIES

If a young woman dreams of pies, it is possible that she will become a flirt. For other people, pie-eating may be warning you of enemies. See also mince pies.

P

PIG

Dreams that feature pigs send a mixed message that if one area of your life is a success, other areas may not be so wonderful. For example, although you may do well in your job, your family life may suffer, and vice versa. See also bacon.

PIGEON

In the language of dreams, a pigeon symbolizes a happy home and family. Some welcome news may also be winging its way toward you soon. If you see pigeons being shot down in your dream, look closely at your own behavior, as you may either be bullying someone who is unable to stand up to you or be treating others unfairly. See also birds.

PILGRIM

Dreaming of becoming a pilgrim indicates success. See also cathedral.

PILLOWS

Small gains are hinted at if the dream pillows are scruffy, otherwise small losses.

PIMPLES

It is not unusual to dream of pimples, either of being covered with them or of seeing them on others. They suggest that you tend to worry over small issues or that other people are nagging you about unimportant matters. See also face.

PINE TREE

Although dreaming of a pine tree has little significance for young dreamers, it hints at good news for older ones. See also trees.

PINEAPPLE

Success is denoted if you dream of a pineapple. See also fruit.

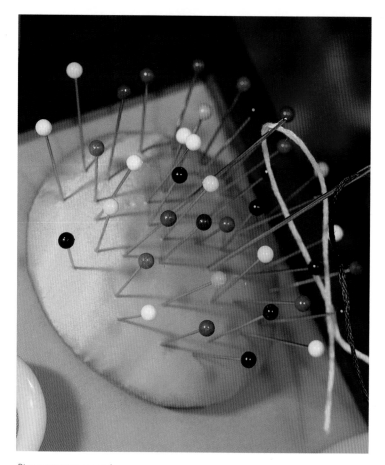

Pins represent quarrels.

PINS

In dream symbolism, pins represent quarrels. See also needles.

PIRATE

If a pirate features in your dream, prepare yourself for exciting times with a number of ups and downs. You may also be going on a journey soon. See also ship.

PIT

As you might imagine, dreaming of a pit is not a positive augury for business people. If you see yourself in a deep pit, a miserable time may be ahead of you. If you see a deep pond that is full of clear water, however, things may soon improve. See also coal mine, ditch, mine, quarry.

P

PITCHER

In general, pitchers denote good friends – even a broken one augurs well for friendship, love, and passion. If you dream of drinking from a pitcher, you may soon become fit and full of vigor.

PLAGUE

If the plague terrorizes your dream, it denotes that your lover or partner may give you a very hard time. See also illness.

PLAY

Watching a play, or being in one, in your dream suggests that a time of fun and laughter is approaching. It may also augur well for success in your career. See also actor, actress, concert, opera, theater.

PLOW

In the long term, a dream plow denotes a successful marriage, although you may put off having children until later in life. In the short term, plenty of work may be looming ahead of you. See also digging, farmer, farming, field, oxen, yoke.

Police in dreams indicate freedom.

Vigor and passion can be found in a dream pitcher.

PLUMS

If plums appear in your dream, they may be encouraging you to push ahead with your plans as the signs are that you may be in the right place at the right time and that everything will therefore work out well. See also fruit.

POLICE

Dreams in which the police appear are usually contrary dreams that denote freedom, happiness, and a rise in status. See also arrest, justice, uniform.

POND

Because water signifies emotion, if you dream of a pond, its condition usually reflects your state of mind, so note whether it was filled with sparkling, clear water or whether it was muddy or full of jagged rocks. See also lake, water.

POTATOES

If you dream of potatoes, the message that they are sending you is that you need to get down to basics and deal with what has to be done. It may be that you have too many things on your plate or that you are need of grounding. Try to identify what is behind, or beneath, your present situation, and then tackle its roots and concentrate on the issues that really need to be sorted out.

Several years ago, I went through a phase of dreaming about potatoes, either in their earthy, natural state or cooked and mashed. In each of these dreams, the potatoes appeared to be menacing me, the whole ones having faces that scowled at me and the mashed ones shaping themselves into monsters that lunged at me. I took note of the dreams, made changes to relieve the pressures that were weighing down on me, and then, I am glad to say, the potato dreams stopped. See also vegetables.

POVERTY

Dreaming of poverty usually hints at a change for the better. See also money, rags, riches.

PRECIPICE

A dream precipice warns you to take care because a disaster may be ahead. See also falling.

PREGNANCY

Potential ideas that you could make good use of, or cash in on, are signified if you dream of pregnancy. See also baby, birth.

PRESENT

See gift.

PRESERVES

If you dream that you are eating preserves, it may foretell a short illness, while making preserves denotes prosperity. See also bread.

PRINCE, PRINCESS

In the language of dreams, princes and princesses hint at a rise in status. See king, palace, queen.

PRISON

Dreaming of a prison may warn you either that mental and physical exertion will be required of you or that you should beware of becoming trapped in a potentially difficult situation. See also convict.

PRIZE

A dream prize points at potential success in your endeavors and growing wealth. See also raffle.

A prize foretells success.

PROFESSOR

Dreaming of listening to a professor giving a lecture signifies learning something new, while being a professor denotes using your talents. See also college, school.

PROPELLER

Unless it is broken, seeing a propeller in your dream hints that your work will go well. See also airplane, boat.

PUB

Dreaming of being in a pub or bar is quite common and denotes future convivial gatherings. See also bar.

PUPPY

According to dream symbolism, a puppy suggests that you will soon make new friends. See also dog.

PURSE

Dreams that feature purses are usually contrary dreams. This is because if the purse is full, you may suffer a small loss, but if it is empty, you may benefit from a modest windfall. See also money, wallet.

PYRAMID

Some dream analysts suggest that a pleasant vacation involving travel is hinted at if you see a pyramid in your dream. If the pyramid is broken, or lying on its side, however, it denotes financial shortages.

QUARRY

In the language of dreams, a quarry warns that you don't know the truth about something or that others may be hiding something from you. See also coal mine, mine, pit.

A quay tells of travel to come.

QUAY

A dream quay often represents travel, especially if boats are tied to it. It may also hint that your wishes will soon come true. See also docks, harbor, ship.

QUEEN

Successful ventures, happiness, honor, and success in your choice of marriage partner are indicated by dream queens. See also cards, coronation, crown, emperor, king, palace, prince, princess.

QUICKSAND

A dream that involves quicksand hardly needs interpreting because its meaning is so obvious: you may in danger of getting yourself into a sticky situation that will be difficult to extract yourself from.

R

RABBI

Dreams that involve a rabbi are not as uncommon as you might suppose, and mean that you probably need an advisor, teacher, or mentor. They may also indicate that you should behave in an honest and upright manner.

RABBIT

A dream rabbit denotes happiness in all of your relationships, whether they are to do with love, friendship, or family. Dreaming of a rabbit is auspicious for those who want to have children. See also hare.

RADISHES

In the language of dreams, radishes are quite a good omen for money, and may indicate a small windfall. If you dream that you are eating them, however, someone may soon behave in a thoughtless or inconsiderate manner toward you. See also vegetables.

A railroad is a metaphor for life.

RAFFLE

Dreaming of winning a raffle is a contrary dream that warns you against taking unnecessary chances or stupid gambles. See also prize.

RAGS

If you see yourself dressed in rags in your dream, it suggests that you can improve your circumstances if you make the effort. See also clothing, poverty.

RAILROAD

Depending on the circumstances of the dream, dreams that feature railroads have lots of potential meanings and reveal what is on your mind. For instance, if the track is clear, it indicates that you should go ahead with your plans, but if it is obstructed, you may need to clear a few obstructions out of your life before you can move forward. If you dream of riding in a train, you may soon be visiting friends. If you are working on a railroad, it suggests that many things need to be done and that a period of hard work is inevitable. If you see yourself walking

R

Rain dreams have many meanings.

along a rail, you may have to walk a "tightrope" in some area of your life. See also train.

RAIN

There are many interpretations of dreams that feature rain, and these depend on the type of rain in your dream and how it affects your dreaming self.

If you are happily walking along on a hot day and are suddenly caught in a light, refreshing shower, it suggests that any minor troubles that you may have will soon be rinsed away. (It also augurs well for those who want to travel on, or over, water.) If you are caught in a downpour, however, it may mean that you are unprepared in some way or are likely to be caught unawares. Torrential rain that causes no damage indicates that although you have rivals or enemies, they won't be able to harm you. Dreaming that your house is leaking during a spell of heavy rain suggests that you are up to something that you ought

not to be, and if the leak makes a real mess, you will probably be caught out. If a woman dreams that her clothing has been soaked in a deluge, it denotes that she may be about to embark on an illicit affair and that she may be found out. If it rains on farm animals, future prosperity is hinted at. See also shower, sky, storm, umbrella, water.

RAINBOW

Your circumstances may soon improve if you dream of a rainbow. See also sky.

RAM

In dream analysis, a ram symbolizes powerful friends. If the ram threatens you, however, your luck could be about to run out. Alternatively, a dream ram may be telling you that someone born under the zodiacal sign of Aries may become important to you in the near future. See also sheep, shepherds.

R

RAPE

There are many possible interpretations of rape dreams. At best, they may signify that someone may soon take advantage of you, while at worst, they may be a predictive warning. If you are living in a household or area where you suspect that someone may suddenly turn nasty, or if you tend to walk through unsafe districts alone, you would be well advised to be especially careful. See also attack, sex.

RASPBERRIES

Dream raspberries represent gossip. See also fruit.

RAT

If a rat features in your dream, it may be warning you that a supposed friend is working against you, that neighbors may be deceiving or taking advantage of you, or that you should beware of becoming entangled with an unscrupulous person. See also mouse, vermin.

RAVEN

Along with crows and magpies, if ravens appear in your dream, they often indicate that you may soon be hearing of a death. See also birds.

RAZOR

In dream symbolism, a razor signifies disagreements and quarrels and warns you not to become involved in other people's disputes. See also barber, beard.

REMOVAL

Dreams of moving house suggest that you will soon have visitors. See also home, house.

RENT

Dreaming of renting property foretells business dealings and contracts. Although you should take care if you dream that you can't manage to pay the rent, dreams that involve renting usually hint at success. See also house.

REVENGE

If the theme of your dream is revenge, you may be feeling the need to hit back at someone who has hurt you.

RHINOCEROS

In the symbolism of dreams, a rhinoceros has sexual connotations, so if you dream of one, your sex life may be about to become exciting.

RHUBARB

You may soon make up with someone whom you have fallen out with if you dream of rhubarb. See also fruit.

R

RICE

In dreams, rice is a symbol of fertility that also promises a happy home life and prosperity. If the rice is dirty or moldy, however, it may denote illness in the family or falling out with a friend.

RICHES

Dreaming of becoming rich suggests that you are about to come into some money. Although you may not become rich, you may nevertheless enjoy an increase in your income. See also abundance, affluence, money, poverty, treasure.

RING

To be given a ring in a dream augurs well for love as it denotes that your lover is sincere. Losing a ring is not so auspicious, however, while dreaming about a broken ring represents a romance that will not last, and if a ring falls off your finger, it almost certainly signifies the end of a relationship. Dreaming of wearing rings, however, presages future prosperity. Some older sources of dream meanings connect rings with eyesight, so if you dream of rings, it may be worth having your eyes tested. See also engagement ring, jewelry.

RIVER

If the river in your dream is flowing gently, and if it is clean and clear, it denotes that happiness is just around the corner (this is a specially positive omen of prosperity for business people or farmers). If the river is muddy or turbulent, however, it warns that you may soon be surrounded by jealousy. If you have any kind of legal battle ahead, dreaming of a river augurs well for success. See also canal, drowning, flood, water.

R

The dream road represents your future life.

ROAD

The condition of the road in your dream is important: if it is wide and obstacle-free, it signifies that your path in life should be easy; if it becomes narrow and stony, however, rough times may be ahead of you. See also milestone, path, signpost.

ROBBER

A dream that features a robber is usually telling you to beware of theft, loss, or deception, so you would be well advised to take steps to protect your home, your possessions, and yourself.

ROCKS

In the language of dreams, rocks signify both danger and hard times. See also stones.

ROOF

A dream roof hints at future celebrations. See also house.

ROOM

Dreaming of a room in a house is both extremely common and very important because the room represents an aspect of your personality or situation. The kitchen relates to household matters and the bedroom to close relationships, while the attic and basement represent memories. If the room is in a mess, it may be warning you that your life is becoming chaotic. If it is clean, tidy, and well furnished, however, it indicates that you are doing well. See also attic, house, kitchen.

Protect yourself from robbers!

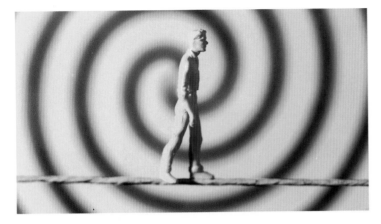

In dreams, ropes have a variety of meanings.

ROPES

The interpretation of a dream rope depends on what is happening in the dream, although generally speaking, dreaming of ropes denotes complications and difficulties.

If you are climbing a rope in your dream, it hints that you will overcome your problems, while if you descending a rope, it indicates that you may not be able to do so. If you are tied up with rope, your life may be restricted in some way, but if you sever the rope, you should be able to break free. Tying up other people or animals with rope suggests that you may be able to control others. Walking a tightrope suggests that although life won't be easy, you should get there in the end, while a skipping rope denotes selfish behavior on your part and tripping over a rope a pleasant surprise. Hanging a rope from a window to enable someone to climb up it indicates a secret love affair.

ROSE

Unless it is wilting, when it symbolizes dying love, dreaming of a rose presages love, prosperity, and social success. See also flowers.

RUBBISH

See trash.

RUBY

In the language of dreams, a ruby means luck in love, gambling, or business. If you dream that a ruby is lost, you may be losing interest in a lover. See also gems.

RUINS

Dreaming of ruins literally warns of impending ruin, so if you are worried about your work, relationship, or anything else, a dream ruin does not generally augur well. Dreaming of an ancient ruin, however, might hint at a sightseeing trip.

RUNNING

Dreaming of running is common, and often forms part of a nightmare in which you can't quite reach your objective. Running in dreams is usually the unconscious mind's way of telling you that you have many obstacles to overcome before you can reach your goal.

RYE

Dreaming of eating ryebread denotes popularity with the opposite sex. See also bread, corn.

Dream roses bring love, prosperity, and success.

S

SACK

If your dream involves a sack something unexpected may be around the corner. See also bag.

SADDLE

An enjoyable and profitable trip is hinted at if you dream of a saddle. See also horse.

SAFE

In dream symbolism, a safe signifies security. See also storehouse.

SAILING

As long as the sea on which you are sailing is calm, sailing dreams denote enjoyable journeys and happy times. If it is rough, however, trouble may be looming. See also boat, ship, water, yacht.

SAILOR

If a woman dreams of a sailor, she may fall in love with a shy man. See also boat, crew, ship, water.

SALAD

Sickness and quarrels are indicated if you dream of a salad. See also vegetables.

SALMON

Dreaming of salmon suggests that you may see something of the world before you eventually settle down. See also fish.

SALT

In many cultures, salt is regarded as protective because it preserves meat and is often said to drive off the devil and other evil influences, so if you dream of salt, it may symbolize protection of some sort. See also pepper, vinegar.

Saucepan dreams tell of battles ahead.

SAUCEPAN

There may be some battles ahead if a saucepan features in your dream. See also boil, boiling, kitchen.

SAPPHIRE

A dream sapphire hints that you may find the right lover. See also gems.

SARDINES

Dreaming of sardines may be warning you not fall for an unsuitable lover. See also fish.

SATAN

See devil.

SAW

If your dream involves a saw, it may indicate that you will be energetic and busy, and that your domestic life will be happy. Although a rusty or broken saw sometimes denotes accidents, it augurs quite well for money matters. See also log.

S

SCHOOL

You may be feeling the need for further education if you dream of a school, although if it is your childhood school, you would be advised to mull over past incidents in your mind and to try to resolve them. Dreaming of a teacher denotes probable success in educational matters. See also blackboard, college, professor.

SCISSORS

Quarrels and partings are signified by dream scissors. See also barber, shears.

SCORPION

Unless you kill the scorpion in your dream, in which case you may overcome your enemies, scorpions in dreams symbolize the danger posed by treacherous friends. Alternatively, a dream scorpion may signify that someone born under the zodiacal sign of Scorpio may soon become important to you.

School dreams denote a need for more education.

SCYTHE

Disappointments in both business and love are possible when you dream of a scythe.

SEEDS

In the language of dreams, seeds represent great future potential. See also fruit, nuts.

SEWING

Sewing dreams indicate a peaceful home. See also embroidery, knitting, needle, tailor, thimble.

SEX

Everybody dreams of sex, and such dreams are often the body's way of checking that it is still in working order. (Don't worry if you dream of strange or kinky sex, sex with someone of your own sex, or sex in front of an audience, as these scenarios are relatively meaningless.) In addition, if you are feeling starved of sex, such dreams help your mind and body to cope with the situation. If you find yourself regularly dreaming about sex, it is probably time for you to find a loving partner with whom to share your needs and emotions. See also genitals, rape.

S

SHADOW

Legal affairs that should turn out well are denoted by dreams in which shadows feature.

SHARK

In dream symbolism, sharks represent enemies, so if a shark attacks you in your dream, it is telling you to beware of a physical or mental attack in your waking life. Even if the shark doesn't attack you, you should still be on your guard against jealous or destructive people.

SHEARS

Dreaming of shears may be highlighting a miserly streak in your nature and may be advising you to consider your behavior toward other people. See also scissors.

SHEEP, SHEPHERD

Prosperity and successful enterprises are denoted if the sheep look healthy in your dream, while flocks of sheep augur especially well for people who work with animals, as well as academics and teachers. If the sheep are sick or scrawny, however, a smaller measure of success is indicated. See also lamb, ram.

Sheep dreams signal success.

SHELLS

In the language of dreams, shells symbolize extravagance.

SHIP

Dreaming of a ship hints at an unexpected promotion or rise in status. If you dream of a shipwreck, however, your financial and business affairs may in danger of collapsing and friends may let you down badly. If you dream of steering a ship through stormy waters, it signifies that you may sail through a difficult situation successfully. See also crew, docks, ferry, harbor, gangway, mast, navy, ocean, pirate, quay.

SHIRT

Having consulted some old sources of dream meanings, it seems to me that you would be well advised to avoid dreaming about shirts. For instance, one interpretation states that if you dream of putting on a shirt, you may break up with your lover as a result of your faithlessness. Another says that if you dream that you are wearing a dirty shirt, you may catch a contagious disease. See also clothes.

SHOES

If you dream of shoes, your unconscious mind may be telling you that you should walk in someone else's shoes for a while, that is, that you should try to see things from another's point of view. Dirty shoes augur badly for business. See also barefoot, clothes, feet, walking.

S

SHOOTING STAR

Success of every kind is hinted at if a shooting star streaks across your dream. See also comet, meteor, sky, star.

SHOP

See store.

SHOWER

Be it a bathroom shower or a shower of rain, a shower denotes creativity and possible success in an artistic or musical venture, especially if you are caught in a rain shower. See also bath, bathing, rain, umbrella.

SIEVE

If you dream of a sieve, something may be slipping away from you.

SIGNPOST

A dream signpost often shows the way to something, and the rest of your dream may tell you what it is. Alternatively, it may signify that you will have to wait for something to happen that will point you in the right direction. See also crossroads, milestone, road.

SILK

Dreaming of wearing silk clothes generally indicates that your circumstances may greatly improve and that you should achieve your aims. Dreaming of wearing old silk often denotes wealth and happiness in old age. See also clothes, lace, velvet.

Note the direction on the dream signpost.

S

SILVER

If you dream of silver coins, future losses may be denoted, especially if you take chances or gamble in your waking life. Although larger items of silverware also signify losses, they suggest that you should be able to recover. See also gold, jewelry, money.

SINGING

Hearing singing in a dream is common and hints that you will be happy in the near future. In addition, if you need help or advice, it may be forthcoming.

SISTERS

Some dream interpreters believe that dreaming of your brothers and sisters indicates that they will have a long life. See also brothers.

SKATING

Skating dreams may be warning you that you are literally skating on thin ice. See also ice.

SKELETON, SKULL

In the language of dreams, a skeleton or skull denotes some sort of trouble, be it in the home, at work, or elsewhere. A grinning skull may signify that someone is jealous of you. See also death.

Smoke dreams spell danger.

SKY

Dreaming of a night sky indicates temporary difficulties, while dreaming of a stormy sky signifies that sweeping changes may be on the way. Alternatively, dreaming of the sky may be advising you that you should aim high if you want to achieve your ambitions. See also clouds, moon, night, observatory, parachute, rain, rainbow, shooting star, star, sun, telescope.

SLEDGE

If you dream of a sledge or toboggan, you may find yourself traveling or having an adventure soon, although you should also beware of sliding into trouble. See also snow.

SLEEVE

A dream sleeve denotes travel. See also arm, clothes.

SMOKE

Whether you are concerned about love, business, or someone's life, dreaming of smoke is a bad augury. Many dream interpreters believe that seeing slowly twisting smoke in a dream presages death. See also fire, flame, match.

Dream skulls can imply jealousy.

S

SNAKE

There are many possible interpretations of snake dreams, and the most compelling one is that someone is jealous of you, or hates you, and that they may do you harm if they get the opportunity.

If you kill the snake in your dream, it has a more positive significance, in that it suggests that you will overcome your enemies. If a snake bites you, or coils itself around you, illness or other unavoidable troubles are denoted. Seeing children playing with snakes is sign that they are being threatened with danger, so you would be advised to take extra care of your children if you have them. In addition, because snakes have a sexual connotation, the dream may be warning you not to become involved in a sexual relationship with someone who will bring you nothing but trouble. See also adder, eels, viper.

In dreams, snow refers to a problem.

SNOW

Some dream interpreters believe that snow represents disappointments and minor illnesses. If you see the sun shining on a snowy landscape, it suggests that you will overcome your difficulties, but dirty snow in any form warns that your problems will get the better of you. See also glacier, ice, sledge.

SOAP

You may soon have to unravel a mystery or puzzle if soap features in your dream. See also bath, bathing, washing.

SOLDIER

If a young woman dreams of a soldier, it hints that a strong, brave, and handsome lover may soon appear on the scene. For other dreamers, a soldier suggests that their battles will be won. See also army, battle, marching, uniform.

S

SOLICITOR

See attorney, lawyer.

SPARROW

You may have to cope with a problem on your own if a sparrow flits into your dream. It may also signify that although your troubles are not that significant, there are many of them to deal with. See also bird.

SPIDER

In the language of dreams, a spider denotes good fortune, especially in relation to your job or business. See also web.

SPIRIT, SPECTER

See ghost, ghoul.

SPONGE

You may have an admirer if you dream of a sponge. See bath, bathing.

SPRING

Dreams of spring or winter are often thought to presage marriage or a partnership in love.

SPY

Dreaming of a spy may be warning you that you should keep a look out for something.

SQUINT

Seeing a person who has a squint in a dream may signify that someone close to you is not a nice person and, more generally, that you should choose your friends with care. See also eyes.

SQUIRREL

A dream squirrel suggests that although you may work hard, you may never be wealthy, but that you should nevertheless be happy and loved by your family.

Ups and downs are represented by stairs.

STABLE

Good fortune and a comfortable home are signified by a dream stable, although a burning stable denotes change. See also horse.

STAG

If you are a woman, a strong and handsome lover may soon come into your life if you dream of a stag. See also deer.

STAIRS, STEPS

Dreaming of stairs is not unusual. If you are going up the stairs, it is likely that your fortunes will improve, but if you are going down them, you could be in for a hard time. If you fall down the stairs, you may become the object of envy and hatred, while sitting on the stairs denotes a gradual improvement in your circumstances. See also escalator, ladder, path.

STAR

Travel and love are indicated if you dream of stars, as well as prosperity and good health. See also meteor, moon, night, observatory, shooting star, sky, zodiac.

A statue foretells a parting.

STATUE

If a statue features in your dream, it may be presaging a parting from your lover.

STONES

If you throw a stone in your dream, it may signify that you lack compassion for others. By the same token, if someone throws a stone at you, it may indicate that they have no compassion for you. See also rocks.

STORE

If you dream of a well-run, profitable store, it denotes your own success, but if it is chaotic, or lacks customers, it may denote that you should reevaluate your lifestyle. See also market.

STOREHOUSE

Future prosperity is hinted at if the dream storehouse is full of goods, but if it is empty, it warns of failure and quarrels. If you dream that a store is burning, it augurs extremely well for the prosperity of your business. See also safe.

STORM

Dangers and difficulties may lie ahead if a storm features in your dream. See also hurricane, lightning, rain, thunder, thunderbolt, wind.

SUITCASE

See luggage.

SUN

In the language of dreams, a blazing sun hints that your efforts will be rewarded by success and that an illness will be followed by a recovery. A rising sun denotes an improvement in your circumstances. If the sun is passing in and out of clouds in your dream, your fortunes may be mixed, however. See also moon, sky, zodiac.

Storms warn of danger.

S

SUNSHADE

Happiness and an increase in your finances are suggested if you dream of a sunshade. See also umbrella.

SURGEON

In dream symbolism, a surgeon represents minor ailments. See also doctor, hospital, knife, operation.

SWAN

If you dream of a swan, it may denote an upturn in your business or financial affairs. See also birds.

SWEARING

Dreams of swearing, or of being sworn at, indicate arguments within the family.

SWEEPING

If you dream that you are sweeping the house, your family life is likely to be happy. See also broom.

SWIMMING

The meaning of a swimming dream depends on its circumstances. For example, if you are swimming along lazily, your life may be quite easy in the future, but if you are struggling against a strong current, a battle may be on the horizon. See also drowning, water.

SWING

If a swing features in your dream, it may hint at either gifts or small changes in plan.

SWORDS

Like all weapons, swords warn of enemies and danger in the language of dreams. See also dagger, knife.

SYRINGE

In a dream scenario, a syringe signifies a false alarm of some kind, like worrying about an illness that may turn out not to be serious. See also drugs, medicine.

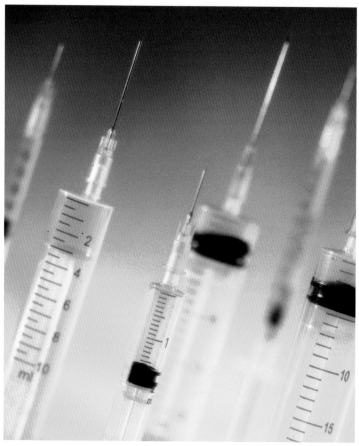

Taxi dreams augur well for work, but you must keep secrets.

TABLE

If you dream of a table, its significance depends on the table's condition. An isolated table suggests a peaceful future, while one that is laden with food denotes happy gatherings. A dirty or broken table, however, indicates losses and possibly also family arguments. See also chair, furniture.

TACKS

Dreaming of tacks or small nails may be telling you to guard against making thoughtless, sarcastic, or hurtful remarks to others.

TAILOR

If a young woman dreams of a tailor, it may signify that she will marry beneath her. Otherwise, a dream tailor warns of misunderstandings and a wasted journey. See also clothes, needle, sewing, thimble.

TALKING

Hearing people talking in dreams is common, and may denote that spiritual help is at hand.

TAP

See faucet.

TAROT

If you see a specific tarot card in a dream, you would be well advised to look up its meaning in a specialized book on tarot. If you see a deck of tarot cards, you may benefit from a tarot reading. See also cards.

TAXI

Dreaming of riding in a taxi during the day suggests that your work will be enjoyable and that others will help you, but if you dream that you are riding in one at night, it may be warning you that you must keep a secret. See also automobile.

Seek out a tarot reader now!

T

Dream tea is great for friendship.

TEA, TEAPOT, TEACUPS

Friendship and harmless gossip or chat are denoted by tea, a teapot, or teacups. If you see dregs in a teacup, however, disappointment in love may be signified. See also coffee, coffee mill, coffee shop, kettle, cup.

TEETH

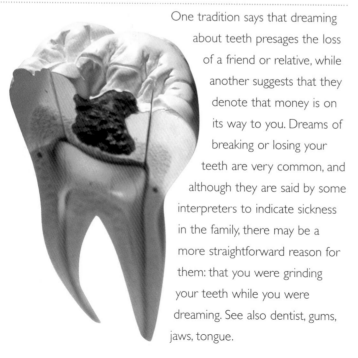

One tradition says that dreaming about teeth presages the loss of a friend or relative, while another suggests that they denote that money is on its way to you. Dreams of breaking or losing your teeth are very common, and although they are said by some interpreters to indicate sickness in the family, there may be a more straightforward reason for them: that you were grinding your teeth while you were dreaming. See also dentist, gums, jaws, tongue.

TELEPHONE, TELEGRAM

You may soon receive some interesting news if a telephone or telegram features in your dream.

TELESCOPE

In the language of dreams, a telescope signifies a journey. See also sky.

TENT

Seeing a tent in your dream indicates that a period of aggravating instability is on the way, perhaps through moving house or traveling. See also camp.

THEATER

Caution is advised if you dream about a theater, specifically guarding against speaking too openly about your plans. See also actor, actress, play.

Don't speak openly in this theater . . .

T

Thimbles mean busy times ahead.

THEFT, THIEF

See robber.

THIMBLE

A busy time may be presaged if you dream about a thimble. If you lose a thimble in your dream, you may incur some small losses. See also needle, sewing, tailor.

THUNDER

Dreaming of thunder often warns against upsetting people who have authority over you. See also lightning, storm, thunderbolt.

THUNDERBOLT

A problem may come out of the blue if a thunderbolt strikes your dream. See also lightning, storm, thunder.

TIGER

In dream symbolism, a tiger signifies being threatened by a hidden danger.

TOAD

Losses and problems are usually denoted by dream toads, but if the toad hops away, it suggests that you will overcome them quite easily. See also frog.

TOBACCO

You may be wasting time or money if tobacco features in your dream. See also match.

TOBOGGAN

See sledge.

TOMB

See grave.

TONGUE

In the language of dreams, a tongue represents scandal or careless talk. See also teeth.

TORTOISE

In Chinese tradition, the tortoise is an omen of long life, but in other traditions it signifies hard work and perseverance.

TORTURE

A dream of being tortured, or of torturing someone else, indicates that you may be torturing yourself in your waking life. See also agony.

TOWER

If the tower is intact in your dream, it hints that your life may soon improve. If it is ruined, however, it usually denotes trouble.

T

TRAIN

Friends may let you down if a train features in your dream. Alternatively, you may be facing an important journey; if so, and if it is connected with business, it suggests that although you will have a struggle, you will probably succeed. See also railroad.

TRASH

If trash features in your dream, it may be advising you that your life is too full and that you should throw out the "trash."

TREASURE

If you dream of finding treasure, your financial position may improve, but if you dream of losing it, the opposite is indicated. See also gems, money, valuables.

TREES

In dream symbolism, healthy trees are a sign of growth and prosperity, but withered or dying trees suggest that you should consider another way of earning money because you are unlikely to succeed as things stand. Dreaming of cutting down a tree may signify that whatever it is that you are trying to do at moment, it is a real waste of time. See also blossoms, forest, garden, log, oak, olives, orchard, palm tree, pine tree, yew tree.

TROUT

Your troubles may soon vanish if a trout features in your dream. See also fish.

TULIP

Some dream interpreters suggest that a tulip signals a hasty, secret marriage. See also flowers.

TUNNEL

Dreaming of a tunnel often warns that if someone close to you is sick in your waking life, they will need to muster all of their effort in order to pull through.

TWINS

Dream twins suggest that you may have to work hard in order to keep yourself and others. They may also indicate that someone born under the zodiacal sign of Gemini may become important to you in the future. See also children.

Even in dreams, twins spell hard work.

U

U.F.O.

Unexpected encounters are presaged if an unidentified flying object puts in an appearance in your dream.

ULCER

In dream symbolism, an ulcer warns of losing friends. See also illness.

Umbrella dreams warn of misunderstandings

UMBRELLA

You may soon be beset by petty annoyances if you dream of an umbrella. Alternatively, trouble could result from a misunderstanding. If you dream that you lend an umbrella to someone, be warned that friends may cost you money. See also rain, shower, sunshade.

UNCLE

A good male friend may soon come to your aid if you dream of an uncle. See also aunt.

UNDRESSING

In the language of dreams, undressing in any way signals that a lack of foresight may cause you problems. See also clothes, nakedness.

Uniforms signify love, passion, and friendship.

UNIFORM

A dream uniform suggests influential friends, although if a uniform features in a young woman's dream, it often indicates love and passion. See also army, police, soldier.

URINATION

Oddly enough, dreaming of urination may be telling you to put your creativity to good use. Usually, however, your body is simply trying to alert you to the fact that you really do need to empty your bladder. See also water.

URN

In the language of dreams, an urn symbolizes prosperity.

Dreaming of a vacation advises you to take some time out.

VACATION

The message sent by dreaming of a vacation is simple: you need a break. See also sunshade.

VALENTINE

If you dream of a valentine, a former lover may get in touch with you. See also love.

VALLEY

On a personal level, a dream valley suggests restrictions and poor health. Dreaming of a valley augurs well for business matters, however, that is, unless it is muddy and wet.

VALUABLES

Dreaming of owning, or being given, valuables is auspicious, but dreaming of losing them, or having them stolen, is an indication that your partnership or marriage may be in trouble. (Oddly enough, divorce often follows theft in waking life.) See also jewelry, treasure.

VAMPIRE

Be careful whom you bestow your love on if you dream of a vampire, because he or she could turn out to be a "bloodsucker" or parasite. See also blood, monster.

VEGETABLES

Dreaming of vegetables signals that you should persevere: although you may experience ups and downs in the near future, as long as you don't give up, you are likely to be successful. Dream vegetables also indicate that you should concentrate on the essentials and ignore unimportant things. See also asparagus, beans, carrots, cauliflower, cucumber, garden, garlic, mushrooms, onions, peas, pepper, potatoes, radishes, salad.

VEHICLE

If you have had a setback in your waking life and dream of buying a vehicle, recovery is signified, but if you dream of selling a vehicle, you may not attain your previous position. Dreaming of riding in a vehicle indicates loss or sickness, while being thrown from one warns of failure. See also automobile, wagon, wheel.

VELVET

Dreaming of velvet generally hints that you will rise in status, but the color of the velvet is particularly relevant. Red denotes passion, while blue represents peace. Yellow velvet hints at fun and entertainment, while white signals sadness. Black velvet foretells bad news, and green prosperity, while orange velvet suggests that you will find the strength to carry on. See also clothes, silk.

Vehicle dreams have a variety of meanings.

V

VERANDAH

If the verandah in your dream is new and freshly painted, it suggests happiness in love and marriage, while a decrepit one denotes romantic and business disappointments. See also house, gallery.

VERMIN

In dreams, any kind of vermin signifies minor ailments. See also beetles, mouse, rat.

VILLAGE

A change for the better may be around the corner if you dream of a village. See also city, cottage.

VINEGAR

Deception may be in the air if you dream of vinegar, and you would be well advised to keep an eye on your lover. See also salt.

VINES

In the language of dreams, vines represent abundance. See also grapes.

VIOLETS

In dreams, violets are symbols of true love and great affection. See also flowers.

VIOLIN

Happiness, harmony, love, and festivities are hinted at if you dream of a violin.

VIPER

A dream viper warns that someone may ruin your work. See also adder, snake.

VIRGIN

Dreaming of a virgin generally presages good luck, while dreaming of the Virgin Mary augurs especially well if you

A change for the better is signified by a dream village.

have been ill or feeling downhearted, because it indicates that you will soon be feeling much better.

VISITING, VISITORS

Dreams of visiting or visitors, be they happy or fraught, usually presage precisely that. See also guests, invitation.

VOLCANO

An explosive situation may be imminent if a volcano features in your dream.

VOMIT

Dreaming of vomit signifies that you are sick of something in your life and that you need to make some changes because the continued stress will make you ill. See also illness.

VOYAGE

See journey.

VULTURE

In the language of dreams, a vulture warns of a dangerous opponent. If you kill the vulture in your dream, however, it is likely that you will overcome them. See also birds.

A violin denotes harmony.

WADING

If the water in which you are wading in your dream is clear, it augurs well for you and your lover; if it is muddy, however, you may soon face some problems. See also water.

WAGON

Dreaming of driving a wagon indicates financial losses, although gains are suggested if a laden wagon arrives at your house. See also automobile, horse, vehicle, wheel.

WAGES

If you receive wages in your dream, you would be advised to keep a careful eye on financial matters. See also money.

WAITER

You may soon have to take care of someone who is sick if a waiter features in your dream.

A dream waiter foretells that you will soon have to wait upon a sick person.

For a walking dream, the nature of the walk will provide the interpretation.

WALKING

The meaning of a dream that involves walking depends on its circumstances. For instance, if you are enjoying a walk in a picturesque place, it augurs well for your future, but if you are walking through mud, brambles, or an unpleasant area, you may be unhappy. Dreaming of walking for a long time suggests that you will have difficulty finding a job, while if you dream of walking with your lover, you should think twice before rushing into marriage. See also barefoot, feet, shoes.

WALLET

Good news from an unexpected source is signaled by a dream wallet. See also money, purse.

WALLS

In the language of dreams, walls represent obstacles.

WAR

See army, battle.

WASHING

If you dream that you are washing in your dream, it indicates that you may be wishing that you could cleanse your conscience and lead a more upright life. See bath, bathing, soap, water.

WASPS

In dreams, wasps symbolize petty annoyances. See also bees.

WATCH

A dream watch may be warning you either that time is running out or that rivals are surrounding you. See also hourglass.

WATER

In dream symbolism, clean water signifies prosperity and happiness, but muddy or dirty water suggests future unhappiness. If water is coming into your house in your dream, it may be warning you that you should be careful whom you trust. If you find yourself bailing out water from a house or boat in your dream, it is likely that you will have many problems to deal with. Playing with water indicates passion, and having it sprayed on your head is an even stronger indication of passionate love. See also bath, bathing, canal, drowning, flood, fountain, lake, lighthouse, ocean, pond,

A dream watch warns that time may be running out.

rain, river, sailing, sailor, swimming, tap, urination, wading, washing, well, yacht.

WEALTH

See abundance, affluence, riches.

WEAVING

Dreaming of weaving often foretells the arrival of good news. See also web.

WEB

A spider's web augurs well for your future prosperity and travel prospects. See also spider.

In water dreams, the interpretation depends on what the water is doing.

WEDDING

Surprisingly, many dream analysts believe that wedding dreams denote sad news, losses in love, and family problems. See also bride, bridegroom, bridesmaid, confetti, husband, marriage.

WEEDS

Dreaming that weeds are taking over your garden suggests that you have too much work to cope with. See also garden, grass.

WELL

If the water in the dream well is clear, it hints that love is on the way. If it is muddy, however, it warns that you should watch your health. See also water.

WHALE

A postponed wedding may be signified if a whale features in your dream. See also fish.

WHEEL

In the language of dreams, a wheel denotes a change for the better. See also automobile, bicycle, vehicle, wagon.

WHEELBARROW

A dream wheelbarrow hints at marriage and lots of children. See also garden.

WHIP

In dreams, a whip symbolizes good news and affection. See also horse.

WHISTLE

Sad or upsetting news may be imminent if your dream features a whistle. See also dog, football.

In dreams, an open window is better than a closed one.

WILL

Dreaming of making a will suggests either that you may have troubles to face or that other people may be trying to take advantage of you. Dreaming of losing a will augurs badly for business matters. See also death, obituary.

WIND

If a strong wind blows through your dream, it signifies that you may have to overcome a number of trials. See also hurricane, storm.

WINDOW

If the window is open in your dream, it suggests that you will probably solve your problems, but if it is closed, you may soon find yourself facing an unexpected danger, although it is unlikely that it will do you any real harm. See also door, doorbell, glass.

WINTER

See spring.

WITCH

Dreaming of a witch may presage domestic or family difficulties. See also magic, wizard.

WIZARD

In dream symbolism, a wizard often signifies some form of inconvenience or, alternatively, a broken engagement. See also magic, witch.

WOLF

Dreaming of a wolf may be warning you of business losses due to theft or of people taking advantage of you.

WORKMAN

A dream workman signals that although you may have to work hard, it is likely that you will be successful.

A workman means plenty to do.

WORMS

Worm dreams are extremely common and indicate that you are worried about something. See also maggots.

WREATH

A dream wreath denotes weddings and happiness. See also flowers.

WRESTLING

If wrestling features in your dream, it may be telling you that although you may have to fight hard for something, you should ultimately win through.

Use the X-ray dream to see behind the scenes.

A dream of writing tells you to put things right.

WRITING

A dream that features writing may either be advising you to put something right or warning you against speculating or taking chances. See also handwriting, ink, pencil, paper.

X-RAY

In the language of dreams, an X-ray denotes behind-the-scenes changes that may be to your benefit. See also hospital.

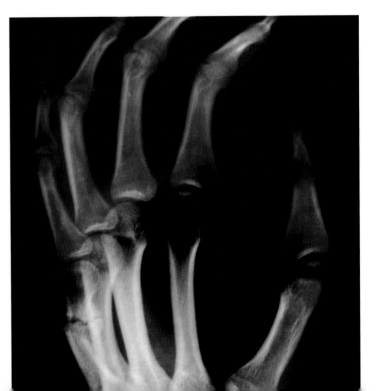

Y

YACHT

Dreaming of a yacht often warns that life may be changeable for a while, as well as somewhat risky. See also boat, water.

YARN

In the language of dreams, yarn (as in knitting yarn), implies a long, happy, and productive life. An old interpretation for a young woman's dream of yarn is that although she may marry someone who is a few steps down the social ladder from her, he will probably turn out to be an excellent husband. See also knitting.

YEARNING

If you dream that you are yearning for something or someone, you are probably doing just that.

YEAST

Sometimes you have to allow matters to take their course, and dreaming of yeast often advises you to let people or situations move at their own pace. See also baker, baking, bread, dough.

In dreams, yew trees refer to old age.

Yarn foretells a happy marriage.

YEW TREE

In dream symbolism, a yew tree signifies old age or older people and may even denote that someone is nearing the end of his or her life. See also cemetery, trees.

YOKE

If a yoke features in your dream, it suggests that you may either willingly choose to fall in with someone else's plans or that you may be forced to do so. See also oxen, plow.

YOLK

One old tradition says that if you dream of the yolk of an egg, you will win the jackpot, so I urge you to try to dream of one! See also eggs.

ZEBRA

A disagreement with friends may be signified by a dream zebra.

ZODIAC

If you dream that you are studying astrology, it suggests that others will soon think well of you, while dreaming of the zodiac foretells a great improvement in your finances. Seeing the constellations of the zodiac approaching you hints at success beyond your wildest dreams, along with fame and fortune. See also moon, star, sun.

ZOO

In the language of dreams, a zoo signifies that a number of options may be opening up to you and that you may find yourself traveling before long.

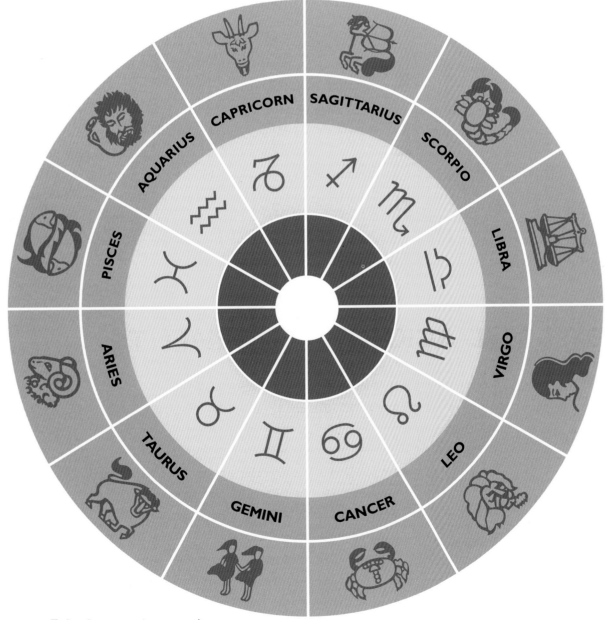

Zodiac dreams promise very good news.

INDEX

CREDITS AND ACKNOWLEDGEMENTS

All Images © Stockbyte except the following:
Images pp 90, 102bl and 111 bl © 2001 Photodisk, Inc

All other photography © D&S Books.
Photographs pp 15l, 20tl, 27tl, 28br, 30bl, 40bl, 42, 43bl, 51tr, 57tr, 76,
79tr, 81tl, 94br, 98 tl, 103 bl by Colin Bowling
Photographs pp88tl and 108tr by Paul Forrester.

(Where b = bottom, l = left, r = right and t = top)